# THE GREEN BERET

## U.S.SPECIAL FORCES
## FROM VIETNAM
## TO DELTA FORCE

D0187830

# VILLARD MILITARY SERIES

# THE GREEN BERET

## U.S. SPECIAL FORCES FROM VIETNAM TO DELTA FORCE

Series Editor: Ashley Brown

Consultant Editors:

Brigadier-General
James L Collins Jr (Retd)

Dr John Pimlott

Brigadier-General
Edwin H Simmons USMC (Retd)

## VILLARD BOOKS  NEW YORK

1986

## Contributing Authors

Adrian English
Jonathan Reed
Leroy Thompson
Ian Westwell


## Acknowledgments

Photographs were supplied by:
Aerospace, Camera Press, Photri, The Photo Source, Popperfoto, The Research House, Rex Features, Frank Spooner Pictures, Leroy Thompson, UPI/Bettman Archive, US Air Force, US Army.

**Front cover photograph:** A Green Beret training at Fort Bragg, North Carolina (US Army/The Research House)
**Back cover photograph:** A Green Beret on a training exercise at Fort Bragg (US Army/The Research House)
**Title page:** Special Forces soldier, Vietnam 1968

Library of Congress Catalog Card Number: 85-40984
ISBN: 0-394-74403-9

Printed in Italy
9 8 7 6 5 4 3 2
First Edition

# CONTENTS

# INTRODUCTION
## The Evolution of US Special Forces

Below: Four members of the 5th Special Forces Group, equipped for mountain climbing, during training at Fort Bragg. The cap badge colours commemorate the unit's service in Vietnam.

IN THE YEARS AFTER World War II, the history of the US Special Forces is the story of a few far-sighted individuals and their fight to overcome the official indifference of the US establishment. After 1945, as the United States and the Soviet Union moved to consolidate their superpower status, the world was torn by wars of insurgency. Faced with the apparent need to create an unconventional warfare unit, Brigadier-General

Robert McClure tried to get the Pentagon's support for the idea. Although faced by a barrage of criticism, from senior officers who had little time for 'elite' forces and were placing their faith in nuclear weapons, McClure won permission to form the Special Operations Section (SOS) think-tank.

With three ex-Office of Strategic Services officers, Colonels Wendell Fertig, Russell Volckman and Aaron Bank, McClure tried hard to sell the idea. However, the SOS was not given the go-ahead until early 1952; in April, Bank went to Fort Bragg, North Carolina, to establish a base, later known as the Special Warfare School. On 20 June, the 10th Special Forces Group (Airborne) – 10th SFG (Airborne) – was activated. Recruits from the paratroopers, Rangers and a whole range of World War II veterans poured in to begin training under the watchful gaze of several experienced officers. Then, as now, training focused on the development of individual skills within the framework of a small detachment, later to be known as the 'A-Team'. Aware of the need to prepare the volunteers for any eventuality, the training staff attempted to make their programme as realistic as possible. Standards were high and many hopefuls failed to make the grade.

In the early 1960s, the role of the Special Forces underwent a major shift: henceforth the groups would be concerned with counter-insurgency missions. The impetus for this change came from President John F. Kennedy, whose growing concern over the successes of guerrilla move-

Below: US Rangers advance under the cover of a smokescreen during the fighting around Salerno in 1943. The Special Forces regard the US Rangers as one of their antecedents. The Green Berets are expected to perform the same sort of hit-and-run raids that the Rangers carried out in World War II.

7

The Special Forces regard the 1st Special Service Force (1st SSF) as one of its two direct military ancestors (the many US Army Ranger units are the other). The 1st SSF was composed of Canadian and US soldiers who were trained for use in rugged, snow-covered terrain. They were also prepared to conduct hit-and-run operations. In the event, their first operation was to recapture the Aleutian island of Kiska from the Japanese in August 1943. The 1st SSF was then sent to the Mediterranean in late 1943. They distinguished themselves in several battles and during the fighting around Anzio they were nicknamed the 'black devils' by the Germans because of their aggressive night patrolling. The 1st SSF was granted the honour of being the first unit to enter liberated Rome in June 1944. They went on to conduct several raids into southern France as part of Operation Dragoon, the Allied invasion of that region in August 1944. The unit was disbanded in December 1944. Below: Men of the 1st SSF during mountain warfare training in Montana.

ments, particularly in Indochina, had a key impact on the future of the Special Forces. With patronage in high places, the future of the forces was assured. Between the President's visit to Fort Bragg in October 1961 and the end of 1963, four more groups were formed for deployment in Africa, the Middle East, Central and South America, and Southeast Asia. The arrival of the 14th Special Forces Operational Detachment (14th SFOD), part of the 77th SFG (Airborne), in Vietnam during 1957 signalled the beginning of the longest and bloodiest deployment in the history of the Special Forces.

## Detachments began to take direct action against guerrillas

Initially, the Special Forces detachments in-country concentrated on training members of the Army of the Republic of Vietnam (ARVN) in the arts of unconventional warfare at the Commando Training Center at Nha Trang, and tried to avoid combat with the Viet Cong (VC) guerrillas. Their efforts led to the establishment of ARVN Ranger units, but as the North Vietnamese military presence in the South escalated in the early 1960s, Special Forces detachments began to take direct action against guerrillas working in the Central Highlands, along the border with Laos and Cambodia, and in the Mekong Delta.

The campaign in the fetid swamps and jungles of Vietnam concentrated on the battle to wean local tribesmen away from the guerrillas. The CIDG (Civilian Irregular Defense Group) programme, the attempt to win the hearts and minds of the locals and create village-defence units, formed the heart of the Special Forces' efforts throughout the Vietnam War. Thrust into a country riven by ethnic and cultural divisions, where the government feared the creation of armed tribal units and the locals viewed outsiders with

distrust, the Green Berets faced an enormous task, yet by late 1961 over 200 villages, protected by some 12,000 armed Montagnards (highlanders), formed an impressive barrier to guerrillas infiltrating into South Vietnam along the Ho Chi Minh Trail.

When the war moved into a new phase in the mid-1960s, the CIDGs began to take the offensive. Under the direction of Special Forces personnel, strike forces carried out hit-and-run raids and prolonged reconnaissance missions against the enemy. As the CIDG strike camps were widely dispersed in 'hot' areas of guerrilla activity, enemy attacks, usually carried out under the cover of darkness with a suicidal ferocity, were frequent. During the mid-1960s the camps were heavily fortified with Claymore mines, concertina barbed wire, machine guns and double perimeters.

Although the camps were capable of delivering an awesome riposte to an enemy assault, Mobile Strike Forces (Mike Forces) were created under Special Forces' tutelage to provide rapid-reaction units to reinforce bases facing overwhelming guerrilla assault. By 1967, the concept had proved so valuable that five Mike Forces, ranging in size from two to five battalions of Special Forces-led tribesmen, were regularly racing into action to relieve a beleaguered camp or to take the enemy on directly.

Far left: A Special Forces camp at Thien Ngon in Vietnam. The Special Forces base camps were part of a counter-insurgency campaign to bring the war to the enemy in the Central Highlands. Above: Special Forces personnel have also been used as advisers during counter-insurgency campaigns in Latin America.

Waging a prolonged war against a cunning and elusive foe encouraged the Special Forces to form highly specialised reconnaissance units. Named after US states or snakes, the 'recons' were a breed apart. Made up of tough individualists, moulded into a tight-knit community that shunned publicity, they carried the war to the guerrillas on their home ground. Patrolling the jungles for weeks on end, the recons were used to snatch suspects, gather intelligence, lay ambushes to take out VC units and, when called upon, to rescue downed pilots from enemy territory.

## Roadrunner teams, carefully disguised, would hunt down guerrillas

In the mid-1960s members of the 5th SFG (Airborne) were creamed off to form the nucleus of the 'Greek-letter projects': Delta, Omega, Sigma and Gamma. Established between 1964 and 1966, these highly proficient outfits carried out long-range deep-penetration raids to gather intelligence on guerrilla activities. Melting into the jungle, 'Roadrunner' teams (CIDG personnel carefully disguised as the enemy) would hunt down their foe. Teams often waited in ambush to snatch guerrillas and then carried out a speedy withdrawal from their area of operations by helicopter.

When the withdrawal of US forces from Vietnam began in the latter part of the decade, most Special Forces turned their responsibilities over to the ARVN. However, units were still able to carry out missions against the enemy. The most famous raid was the daring attempt to rescue US prisoners of war held at Son Tay in North Vietnam. This mission, in November 1970, was planned down to the minutest detail and executed with perfection, but the prisoners had been moved elsewhere.

Following the Son Tay episode, the Special Forces operations in South Vietnam came to a close. The CIDG programme finished at the end of December, and the various reconnaissance groups were wound down between 1970 and 1972. The final act of the drama occurred in April 1972 when the MACV Special Operations Group (MACV/SOG), the body that coordinated the activities of the Special Forces in Vietnam, was disbanded.

During the phased withdrawal of US forces from Vietnam under the Nixon administration, most SFGs were either redeployed or deactivated. Between 1969 and 1974, four groups were disbanded, while others returned to their original areas of responsibility – Africa, the Middle East, West Germany, Latin America and the Pacific. In a period of sweeping reductions in military expenditure, those groups that remained on station underwent manpower cuts; similar reforms took place in training and back-up facilities.

In the aftermath of these damaging reforms the Special Forces assumed a low profile that was maintained until the early 1980s. But a pointer to the future was provided in late July 1969 when the Special Warfare School was designated the Institute for Military Assistance, a body to coordinate

Top: Mounting instability in the Middle East during the 1970s led to the formation of a special command for use in possible interventions in the region – the Rapid Deployment Joint Task Force. Around 450 Special Forces personnel are earmarked for use by this force.
Above: Special Forces deployment is worldwide – Green Berets on Okinawa.

military support for friendly states. Increasingly, the Special Forces would provide the 'cutting edge' for US strategic policy. Major emphasis was placed on the training and organising of dissident forces in Latin America to combat the perceived threat posed to US security by Soviet-backed regimes such as Cuba and, later, Nicaragua.

The role of the Special Forces also expanded to meet the growing menace of international terrorism in the early 1970s. Presidential pledges to defeat the hijackers and bombers with force, and a resurgence of political confidence in the military, provided the seed-bed for the creation of the 1st SFOD D (Special Forces Operational Detachment Delta) in July 1978. Better known as Delta Force, this highly secretive unit was the brainchild of a Vietnam veteran, Charles Beckwith, who faced considerable difficulties in getting the project off the ground. Delta Force shot to international prominence after Operation Eagle Claw, the audacious but ultimately unsuccessful attempt to rescue US hostages held in Tehran in April 1980.

Despite the failure of the mission, Eagle Claw signalled the US government's willingness to resume a worldwide peace-keeping role. More successfully, members of Delta Force and other Special Forces Groups took part in the 1983 invasion of Grenada, Operation Urgent Fury. The early 1980s also saw a growing awareness of the strategic worth of Special Forces, and in October 1982 the 1st Special Operations Command, a body empowered to improve training standards and coordinate the overseas deployment of units, was established at Fort Bragg.

## Detachments played a key part in combat training Central American armies

The creation of the Rapid Deployment Joint Task Force in the early part of the decade led to increasing cooperation between the 5th SFG (Airborne), deployed in the Middle East, and the Egyptian armed forces, that was most fully expressed in the Bright Star military exercises. Elsewhere, detachments of the 7th SFG (Airborne) played a key part in the combat training of Honduran and Salvadorean forces engaged in protracted campaigns against internal guerrilla groups.

In the years since the Vietnam debacle, the fortunes of the Special Forces have ebbed and flowed in relation to the US government's willingness to accept a dominant part in world affairs. Against a background of superpower confrontation (primarily through the actions of surrogate states such as Syria and Israel), and with the ever-present threat of terrorist outrages, it seems likely that the revitalisation of the Special Forces will continue.

Below: A member of the 7th Special Forces Group trains Liberian soldiers. Green Berets have given training assistance to many armies of the Third World, including Bolivia, Guatemala, Somalia and Sudan.

# 1
# EARNING THE GREEN BERET
## Training and Recruitment

In 1954, a year or so after the formation of the Special Forces, a committee of officers and NCOs met at Fort Bragg in North Carolina and chose the green beret as a suitable headgear for members of the new unit. Based on that of the British Royal Marine Commandos, the beret was first worn publicly in June 1956. The following December, the 77th Special Forces Group (Airborne) ordered all its personnel to wear the beret.

The Special Forces adoption of a distinctive emblem, however, brought them into conflict with senior officers, who ordered the beret to be replaced. Despite a vigorous campaign to retain the beret, the ban remained in force until 1961.

In October 1961 President John F. Kennedy, a keen supporter of Special Forces, visited Fort Bragg and reviewed the 5th and 7th Special Forces Groups. At Kennedy's request, the troops wore the green beret at the ceremony. Believing that the beret would be a suitable mark of distinction, the President then ordered the reinstatement of this Special Forces emblem.

Above: The US Special Forces insignia, as worn on the front of the green beret.

SINCE 1945 most of the world's armed forces have had to adjust to fundamental changes in the art of warfare. In the aftermath of World War II, nationalist movements in various colonial possessions began to employ guerrilla tactics against their colonial masters and few of the major powers were equipped to deal with this threat. It soon became clear that large conventional units were unable to defeat the guerrillas and that small teams of highly-trained specialists were better suited to playing the insurgents at their own game, and winning. The United States was one of the first countries to tap the potential of this new type of fighting man.

Deadly exponents of the new art of unconventional warfare, the men of the US Army Special Forces are tough professionals whose combat skills have been honed to perfection in one of the world's most exhaustive and thorough military training programmes. The few men who get through the course truly earn the right to wear one of the most revered symbols of any crack fighting force – the green beret.

The present-day Special Forces, formed in 1952, can trace their lineage back to the Office of Strategic Services (OSS). Active during World War II, the OSS was instrumental in the creation of guerrilla-style forces to attack and harass the enemy's weak points. One formation in particular, Detachment 101, working with Kachin and Jingpaw tribesmen in Burma, proved the value of such clandestine operations.

The commander of the new unit, designated the 10th Special Forces Group (Airborne), was an OSS veteran, Colonel Aaron Bank. With boundless energy, Bank immediately began to formulate the role of the Special Forces, defining their mission as 'to infiltrate by land, sea or air, deep into enemy-occupied territory and organise the resistance/guerrilla potential to conduct Special Forces operations, with emphasis on guerrilla warfare.' With the help of some early volunteers, Bank developed a training course in unconventional warfare that formed the basis of the present day programme. Bank's original course, however, has been constantly updated to accommodate changes in the type and areas of operations that might be faced by members of the Special Forces.

## Few people realised the importance that counter-insurgency would assume

At the outset very few officers outside the Special Forces base at Fort Bragg in North Carolina were even aware of its existence. Most of those regular army officers who did know about the Special Forces viewed their psychological and guerrilla warfare missions with distrust. The US Army of the 1950s was geared to conventional warfare in Europe rather than unconventional operations, and even the early Special Forces viewed their role in the limited context of behind-the-lines operations in Europe. Few people realised the importance that counter-insurgency would soon assume.

Page 13: A member of the Green Berets on a weapons training course, learning how to handle the AK-47, a favoured rifle of guerrillas the world over. In weapons training, Green Beret specialists learn how to operate over 80 types of small arm.
Left: A member of the 77th Special Forces Group practises abseiling at Camp Hale in Colorado.
Above: Unarmed combat is a staple of training for any elite force, and the Green Berets are no exception to this rule.

However, many early members of Special Forces were especially well-qualified to carry out operations in the Soviet Union's satellite states: many had been born in eastern Europe and had entered the US Army under the Lodge Bill which allowed foreigners to gain American citizenship by serving in the US armed forces.

In September 1953, the 77th Special Forces Group (Airborne) was activated from elements of the 10th SFG (Airborne). Elements of the 10th also became the nucleus of the Special Warfare Center, while the remainder of the unit, some 782 men, deployed to Bad Tolz in West Germany, where they would be closer to the action should war break out.

The 10th SFG (Airborne) in Germany were designed to be ready to move into Hungary, Czechoslovakia, Romania, East Germany or Poland should hostilities break out. As one would expect of troops trained to work with the local population, the Special Forces were soon widely accepted by the Germans in the Alps, who aided the Green Berets against conventional ground troops during military exercises. Even though the US Seventh Army in Germany was well-trained and highly professional, Special Forces-led 'guerrillas' harassed them continuously during these manoeuvres. By the mid-1950s, members of the Special Forces,

Below: Special Forces members have to acquire a complete theoretical knowledge of the equipment they are required to use. Here, the finer points of a para-rig are being explained.

especially the 10th SFG (Airborne), were involved in exchange training programmes with other NATO special units such as the British Special Air Service.

Most US commanders in Germany, however, did not really understand the Special Forces role in any future war. Many would have gladly traded the 'Sneaky Petes' for a few more tanks. As a result, by the mid 1950s, Special Forces strength in Europe had been more than halved to less than 400 men.

Below: Sudden death for a 'guerrilla' on the Green Beret 'manhunt' course. One of the most important parts of training is the simulation of conditions that might occur in the field.

# Earning the Green Beret

Right: Practising in High Altitude, Low Opening gear.
Below: Trainees prepare to emplane in a C-5 Galaxy.
Bottom: Safe landing.

Back at Fort Bragg the 77th SFG (Airborne) continued to train in the skills of guerrilla warfare and psychological operations. By June 1957, elements of the 77th had moved to Okinawa in the Pacific, where they formed the nucleus of the 1st Special Forces Group (Airborne). Just as the 10th SFG (Airborne) specialised in Europe, the 1st SFG (Airborne) trained for service in the Far East. Indeed, the 1st was soon training troops from Vietnam, Thailand, Taiwan and the Philippines. The 1st also established their own jump school on Okinawa to give basic parachute training to American and foreign troops. Although they were still viewed with suspicion by many senior officers, by 1960 the three Special Forces groups had a combined strength of about 2000 hard-core professionals.

In the late 1950s and early 1960s, the Special Forces began to turn their attention to the wars of national liberation – the communist-backed insurgencies taking place in the Third World. As the reigning US experts on guerrilla tactics, it was natural that the Special Forces should become highly proficient in the techniques of anti-guerrilla or counterinsurgency warfare. Since gaining the trust of the population

The arguments for and against the creation of elite forces have been debated in many modern armies since World War II. The creation of specialist units has always been considered necessary – engineers, or artillerymen, for example, clearly need skills that are different from those of the infantryman. And formations such as the British Royal Marines have always considered themselves, because of their range of fighting skills, an elite force. During World War II the British government decided to create a commando force ('leopards' as Churchill described them) to act as a spearhead and raiding formation, with troops whose training and recruitment raised them well above the average, and from this, modern elites are descended. The arguments against such units are that they cream off the best men from line units, and therefore lower the fighting ability of the army as a whole; that they lower morale in line units which are publicly held up to be inferior to the elite force – the whole army should be able to feel itself an elite; and that in a mass war, the clash of hundreds of thousands of men leaves little scope for the heroics of small bodies of men, however brave and determined.

Both the Soviet and US armies were firmly of this negative opinion in the aftermath of World War II – but the prevalence of small-scale guerrilla wars since then has brought about a change in attitudes. Where massive firepower and weight of material cannot carry the day (as in Vietnam and more recently in Afghanistan) then relatively small bodies of men can prove invaluable. The debate will, no doubt, continue; but for the moment, elite forces are very much part of the military establishment of both the US and the Soviet Union.

Above: Two Green Berets learning the delicate art of house clearing – a skill that was much in demand during the Vietnam War.

and, in many cases, training them to defend themselves is an important part of counter-insurgency warfare, the Special Forces ability to work with the indigenous population and provide various types of training made them well-suited for the new counter-insurgency role. However, it was essential that a tougher, more exhaustive training course be devised to prepare the Green Berets for this new sphere of operations.

With the inauguration of President Kennedy in 1961, the US Special Forces gained a supporter in their new Commander-in-Chief, who believed that counter-insurgency operations were vital to the strategic interests of the United States. Kennedy's interest in the Third World was reflected in the

Above: Men of an A-Team on a SERE (Survival, Evasion, Resistance and Escape) course. The Green Berets are armed with M14 rifles, while the man on the right carries a Soviet PPS-43.

formation of the Peace Corps and in the increased size and doployment of Special Forces. To meet the manpower requirements caused by this rapid expansion, the Special Warfare School at Fort Bragg increased the number of its graduates from under 400 to over 3000 per year and developed an even more rigorous training programme.

New recruits, tough and in peak physical condition, are always high-school graduates and some have college degrees. However, there is no direct entry into the Special Forces – candidates are drawn from the US armed forces and, with an average of three years' service behind them, most are in their early 20s. Most are airborne-qualified but few have combat experience. After arriving at Fort Bragg training school, they face one of the most stringent selection courses ever devised: a three-stage programme in which their mental and physical abilities are evaluated. As many as 75 per cent of candidates fail to make the grade.

The first 31 days of the course are given over to developing stamina and basic combat skills. During a 17-hour day, the recruits begin with a six-mile route march, carrying a 45lb pack, and then return to base for more exercises. The day only really begins after this, with instruction in patrolling, survival in hostile territory and living off the land. Although most men are para-qualified, they learn to use the T10 and MC1 parachutes as well as rapelling at a nearby airborne school.

As the Special Forces are primarily deployed in clandestine operations behind enemy lines, great emphasis is placed on SERE (Survival, Evasion, Resistance and Escape) techniques. During this popular course, trainees are put through their paces with a seven-day field exercise in the Uwharrie National Forest. After the 'easy' part of the course, the last three days are devoted to manhunts. Armed only with a knife, the recruit has to survive by living off the land and evading his pursuers. If successful, he is then permitted to embark on the second stage of the training, in which each recruit takes a specialist course in one of five skills.

During the eight-week course in engineering, the recruit is taught the finer points of both construction and destruction. As with all the specialist courses, much of the time is devoted to putting classroom theory into practice. Most days, recruits are on the ranges learning to make explosives from a variety of substances and then use them to deadly effect. To familiarise the prospective demolition experts with potential targets, instructors take their recruits to likely objectives

Below: Special Forces must reach their targets by air, sea, or land, and the ability to arrive silently and undetected on a hostile shore is an essential skill that has to be learned in training.

where they are shown the most vulnerable points. However, the course also involves construction, and trainees are taught how to build bridges, dams and stockades.

## The weapons specialists are familiar with 80 different types of smallarm

The weapons specialists take part in eight weeks of intensive instruction that familiarises them with over 80 different types of modern smallarm. Particular emphasis is placed on marksmanship, and proficiency in the building and use of less conventional weapons such as crossbows. Specialists are also taught the tactical use of their weapons: at squad, platoon and company levels.

As the Special Forces are expected to go 'native' and operate independently for long periods, they also learn how to work with a wide variety of communications equipment. To pass this course candidates have to be capable of sending and receiving Morse code at a minimum rate of 18 words per minute. First rate soldiers are expected to service their equipment in the field and recruits are taught to repair and maintain both transmitting and receiving sets. The disruption of the enemy's communications equipment is also seen as an invaluable skill and prospective specialists have to become adept in this field.

Below: Being able to use scuba diving gear (and also being able to reach a target without leaving a tell-tale trail of air bubbles) is part of the specialist instruction that many members of the Green Berets undergo.

Although the Green Berets' combat experience has been in the form of counter-insurgency warfare, at the time of their formation they were intended for use as an unconventional warfare unit. Unconventional warfare was inspired by the activities of Britain's Special Operations Executive and the US Office of Strategic Services during World War II. Although not strictly military units, both these organisations had provided a valuable method of organising and coordinating resistance group activities behind enemy lines.

The Special Forces were particularly interested in this role, for at the beginning they were intended for use in eastern Europe. Green Berets would be infiltrated behind the Warsaw Pact front line to organise anti-communist resistance forces that would strike at rear-echelon units.

The Green Berets' airborne training requirement was introduced because aerial methods were anticipated as the primary means of infiltration. Similarly, the majority of the foreign languages taught were those of eastern Europe. The motto of the Special Forces, 'De Oppresso Liber' (Free the Oppressed), encapsulates this original concept of the Green Berets' employment in unconventional warfare.

Candidates who opt for the medical specialist course undergo the longest and most difficult training programme. Lasting up to 50 weeks, the course trains the men to deal with most types of combat wound. As the Special Forces are expected to wage 'hearts-and-minds' programmes, to win the trust of the indigenous population, they also learn how to cope with more common ailments and diseases. It is believed that candidates work with animals during the programme; if the 'patient' dies, the recruits are thrown out of the Special Forces.

The fifth specialist course concentrates on developing a recruit's intelligence-gathering skills. Particular attention is focused on establishing intelligence networks, the organisation of guerrilla forces and the interrogation of suspects.

Following the completion of the second stage of basic training, the trainees are brought together to learn the operational procedures of Special Forces working in the field. After an initial period of theoretical training at Camp Mackall, the recruits are formed into teams and then dropped into the heart of the Uwharrie forest. Once in position, they have to evade the enemy, in the form of aggressor forces drawn from the 82nd Airborne Division, and form guerrilla units. The guerrillas, a random selection of US soldiers, play the part of untrained 'natives' and the Green Berets are expected to knock them into shape within a month. Capture, or failure to raise a guerrilla force, spells the end of the course for the candidate. The successful completion of the course allows the trainees to wear the much-coveted green beret.

After completing their basic training the Green Berets continue to acquire additional skills during their attachment to US military commands throughout the world. Graduates from the Fort Bragg school are usually cross-trained in some other skill. This is seen as being vital to the performance of Special Forces units operating in the field as the loss of one specialist might jeopardise the other members of the team. As the Green Berets are geared up to conduct missions in any part of the world, each man is also taught the specialist techniques needed to survive in every type of environment.

As the teams are likely to work with indigenous populations, particular emphasis is placed on the teaching of languages and training local forces. In general, at least one member of a Special Forces team should be fluent in the native language. Those teams intended for service in Latin America or Europe find it easier to reach the required level of proficiency than those scheduled for deployment in the Middle East, Africa or Southeast Asia. However, there are now a number of Thai or Vietnamese speakers in the Special Forces because of the Vietnam War.

When involved in organising and training local forces for defence or counter-insurgency operations, each member of the Special Forces team has a particular job. Two officers, the operations sergeant and the two weapons experts attached to each team, teach basic tactics, the use of

Above left: Members of A-Team 743 of the 7th Special Forces Group on an exercise at Fort Bragg in May 1980. They are demonstrating the wide variety of weapons that they can use – an Israeli Uzi sub-machine gun in the foreground, then a US M16 assault rifle, and finally a Soviet AK-47 assault rifle

Left: Camouflage, even of weapons, is one of the critical skills that can mean the difference between life and death for a Green Beret on active service.

Above: A combat engineer with the 7th Special Forces Group, Sergeant John Moran, prepares to destroy his target during a training exercise.

weapons and operational procedures. An intelligence sergeant is on hand to prepare the locals to supply useful information and counter enemy subversion, while the communications expert spends his time training them to use basic radio equipment. The medical specialist instructs the local recruits in rudimentary hygiene and first-aid. As part of the hearts-and-minds aspect of Special Forces operations, the team's engineer is on hand to assist and direct building programmes. In his more warlike capacity, he trains the local forces in the use of explosives and booby traps. Teams are expected to be able to set up and train a battalion-sized counter-insurgency force within a month of making contact.

## Most prefer to concentrate on accuracy and achieving a single-shot kill

The Special Forces' preparations for war continue during peacetime, with members learning the dangerous arts of insertion into enemy-occupied territory. The most common methods used are HALO (High Altitude, Low Opening) and HAHO (High Altitude, High Opening). During a HALO insertion, the Green Beret parachutes from 35,000ft and free-falls to the minimum safety height before opening the parachute canopy. Before trying a real HALO jump, each man is taught the correct procedures for stabilising his parachute in high winds, in a wind tunnel. HAHO is a method of entering enemy territory by gliding down undetected. By dropping at a rate of around half-a-mile per 1000ft of descent, a Green Beret should be able to travel a distance of up to 100km from the jumping-off point.

The Green Berets are also experts at underwater insertions, with most men skilled in the use of Scuba gear. Using the new CCR 1000 system, teams are capable of reaching a target without leaving a tell-tale trail of air bubbles. The gear allows a Green Beret to stay submerged for up to four hours. Individual team members also become highly trained snipers. During a short but intensive course, each student is expected to achieve a kill from 1800ft and learn the essential art of camouflage and concealment. Although most of the pupils are taught to fire several shots in quick succession, most prefer to concentrate on accuracy and achieving a single-shot kill.

Like all elite formations, the Special Forces have placed a high priority on creating the all-round soldier: a man capable of operating both as an individual and as part of a small team. By necessity, the Green Berets' training programme has been specifically created to weed out the poor candidates and identify those men able to cope with the rigours of unconventional warfare and behind-the-lines work. Despite the diversity of basic training, the US Special Forces never rest on their laurels; they are always looking to improve their skills and are prepared to make use of any new combat techniques that become available. Only by maintaining the highest state of readiness can the Green Berets hope to succeed in the twilight world of counter-insurgency.

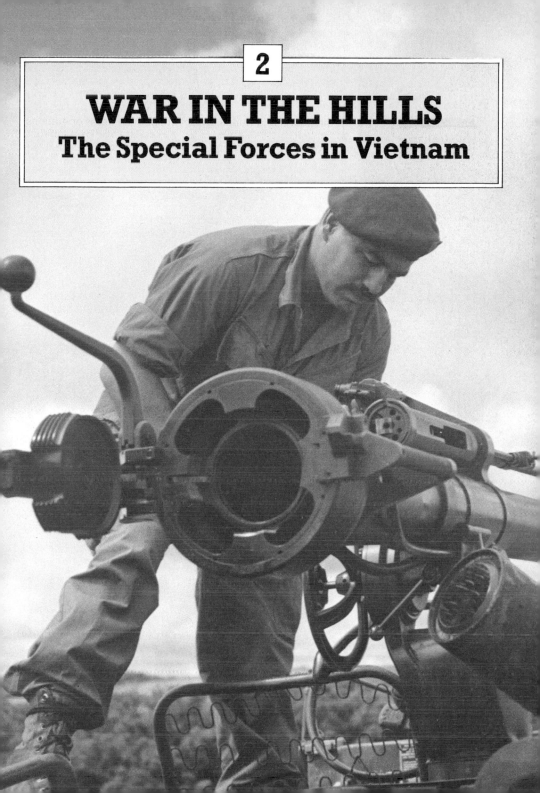

# 2

# WAR IN THE HILLS
## The Special Forces in Vietnam

The involvement of the US Army Special Forces with the tribesmen of Vietnam's Central Highlands began in December 1961 with the establishment of the pilot Village Defense Program at Buon Enao village in Darlac Province. Seven men were detailed, along with a South Vietnamese contingent, to develop a programme of civic action in the area.

In early 1962 a 12-man A-Team from the 1st Special Forces Group (Airborne) – 1st SFG (Airborne) – joined the men at Buon Enao to train the tribesmen in military skills. This campaign was known as the Civilian Irregular Defense Group (CIDG) Program. Further development led to the formation of Headquarters US Army Special Forces (Provisional) Vietnam, to which personnel from the 1st, 5th and 7th SFGs were assigned. So great did the Special Forces' commitment become that, in October 1964, the entire 5th SFG (Airborne) arrived to take control of all Special Forces activity in the war. At the time, the 5th SFG (Airborne) comprised just 951 men, but by July 1966 it had grown to 2627 with a huge indigenous force under command. Above: A CIDG unit shoulder flash.

ONE URGENT priority of the US Army Special Forces in Vietnam was the eradication of Viet Cong (VC) influence among the Montagnard tribesmen of the Central Highlands. Control of this area would, in effect, cut South Vietnam in two, and the VC were taking the opportunity to 'swim freely among the people', in the words of Chairman Mao, recruiting supporters for the communist cause. Since the Montagnards had little reason to trust the South Vietnamese government there was a strong possibility that they could be persuaded to side with the North. For many years the South Vietnamese people and successive governments had discriminated against the fiercely independent hill people, treating them as little more than unsophisticated savages. The US Special Forces, on the other hand, were determined that the Montagnards should become the 'fishermen' who would help them 'net' the communists. To this end, considerable resources of arms, money, medical aid and other material benefits were showered upon the Montagnards to gain their loyalty. The tribesmen, although unused to Western affluence, were quick to accept the incentives.

Once a pioneering group had set civic action programmes in motion in an area, detachments from the US Special Forces and the Vietnamese Special Forces (the Luc Luong Dac Biet, or LLDB) would begin military training. Defensive positions such as stockades and trenches would be built

Page 27: A Special Forces NCO checks over a 106mm recoilless rifle. The relatively light weight of recoilless weapons made them key armaments for both sides during the fighting in the mountains.

Left: A South Vietnamese member of one of the civilian irregular defence groups (commonly known as 'cidgees'), festooned with M60 ammunition belts, prepares for action against the Viet Cong.

Far left: Part of the training course built by Sergeant Edward Cockburn (on left of photograph) at Dong Ba Thin.

around the village, and the men would receive instruction in the use of the M1 carbine and the M3 'grease gun' sub-machine gun. Basic tactics and radio operation were also taught, enabling village defenders to call in reserve strike forces of trained and heavily armed troops that had been organised to garrison the area and carry out patrols.

By the end of 1963, the US Special Forces, with the aid of the LLDB, had trained 18,000 strike force troops and more than 43,000 hamlet militiamen. The Civilian Irregular Defense Group (CIDG) Program, as the campaign among the Montagnards came to be known, had, meanwhile, become the responsibility of Military Assistance Command Vietnam (MACV) as part of Operation Switchback, and Montagnard training periods had been standardised, with strike force personnel receiving six weeks and hamlet militiamen receiving two weeks.

### Early in 1963, 'cidgees' began setting ambushes for the VC

Early in 1963 there was a subtle shift in the thrust of the CIDG Program, as 'cidgees' began to patrol more aggressively, searching out or setting ambushes for the VC rather than passively waiting to respond to attack. In October the Border Surveillance Program (originally known as the 'Trail Watcher Program') came under the CIDGs, and Special Forces-trained irregulars were deployed in patrolling key infiltration routes along the borders of South Vietnam. Thus, a force originally conceived to protect its own villages was quickly

Below: A member of the 5th Special Forces Group training his cidgees in the use of a 105mm howitzer, while the training session is filmed.
Far right: Wading through swamps in Dinh Tuong Province, early in the Vietnam War, a US adviser (carrying a carbine) operates with South Vietnamese forces.

Right: Patrolling one of the dangerous waterways of South Vietnam.
Below right: A purple smoke grenade is used to mark a landing zone for incoming helicopters.

evolving new roles, and the control of large areas from military encampments, together with intelligence-gathering operations, soon took precedence over village-based guard duties.

The majority of the indigenous CIDG personnel came from the populous Rhada tribe of Montagnards, but as the programme expanded it became necessary to establish strongpoints in areas dominated by other minorities. Men were recruited from the ethnic Cambodians within South Vietnam, from such religious sects as the Hoa Hao and the Cao Dai, and from the Nung tribe. The ethnic Chinese Nungs, in particular, proved themselves adept soldiers and were often selected for special missions or vital security duties.

## Special Forces managed to defuse an uprising by appealing to Montagnard loyalty

However, the involvement of new minorities in the CIDG brought its own problems, for traditional animosities existed between the tribes. Moreover, perhaps the strongest hostility lay between the mountain people and the South Vietnamese as a whole, a hostility which led to the 1964 rebellion of Montagnard troops. Although the US Special Forces managed to defuse the uprising in most camps by appealing to Montagnard loyalty to America, some members of the LLDB were killed or injured before peace was restored.

In addition to the conflicts between the LLDB and the Montagnards, the LLDB often came into conflict with the US Special Forces. One cause was the lack of aggressiveness often displayed by the LLDB, earning them the sarcastic title of the 'Look Long Duck Backs'. The LLDB also had a

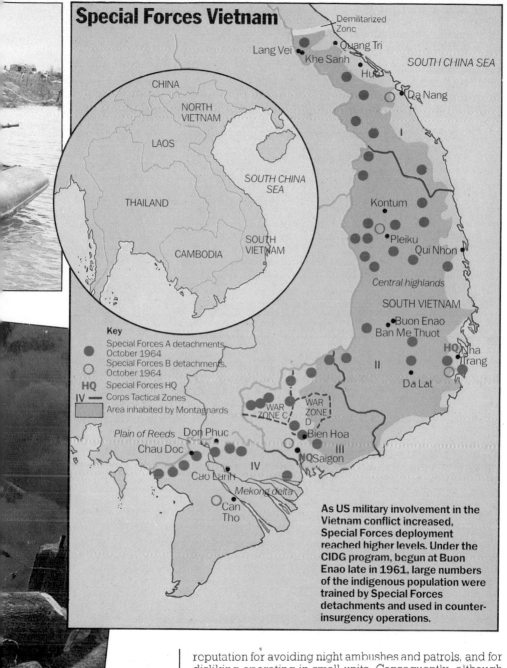

# Special Forces Vietnam

Demilitarized Zone

SOUTH CHINA SEA

Lang Vei
Quang Tri
Khe Sanh
Hue
Da Nang

**CHINA**

**NORTH VIETNAM**

**LAOS**

**SOUTH CHINA SEA**

**THAILAND**

**SOUTH VIETNAM**

**CAMBODIA**

I

Kontum

Pleiku

Qui Nhon

Central highlands

SOUTH VIETNAM

Buon Enao
Ban Me Thuot

HQ Nha Trang

II

Da Lat

## Key

- Special Forces A detachments, October 1964
○ Special Forces B detachments, October 1964
HQ Special Forces HQ
IV — Corps Tactical Zones
Area inhabited by Montagnards

WAR ZONE C
WAR ZONE D

Plain of Reeds
Don Phuc
Bien Hoa
Chau Doc
HQ Saigon
III
IV
Cao Lanh
Mekong delta
Can Tho

As US military involvement in the Vietnam conflict increased, Special Forces deployment reached higher levels. Under the CIDG program, begun at Buon Enao late in 1961, large numbers of the indigenous population were trained by Special Forces detachments and used in counter-insurgency operations.

reputation for avoiding night ambushes and patrols, and for disliking operating in small units. Consequently, although the LLDB were theoretically in command, with the US Special Forces as observers and advisers, the 'advisers' often ended up in combat command. A Green Beret sergeant was frequently seen carrying responsibilities which, in normal circumstances, would fall to an officer of at least the rank of captain.

The build-up of conventional US troops in Vietnam during 1965 and 1966 partly caused the shift by CIDG units towards more offensive operations. Special Forces-trained irregulars often acted as scouts for US Army units and, in the case of airmobile units such as the 1st Air Cavalry and the 173rd Airborne Brigade, the cidgees acted as stalking horses, patrolling in enemy territory until they came under attack; they would then attempt to hold the enemy down until the heavily armed airmobile infantry flew in. The cidgees proved very effective when they were operating under a commander who understood them and how to use them. Unfortunately, most of the US commanders failed to trust the cidgee force and did not employ them correctly, and, under these, the Montagnards enjoyed only very limited success. The more astute of the commanders realised that the greatest value of the CIDG units lay in intelligence gathering, and Montagnards participating in such specialised operations as Projects Delta, Omega, Sigma and Gamma made valuable contributions to their success.

## Mobile guerrillas were inserted into communist occupied positions

The Mobile Strike (Mike) Forces which evolved out of the CIDG Program were widely used in the Greek-letter projects. In 'Blackjack' operations (part of Project Sigma), for example, mobile guerrilla forces were inserted into 'Indian country' – communist-occupied positions – to make a reconnaisance: they would then be reinforced by Mike Force battalions which would exploit the recce's findings to make a strike of the maximum effectiveness. Other Blackjack operations involved raids and sabotage in areas believed safe by the enemy. The reconnaissance platoons used in these raids were the elite of the Mike Forces, and their training was conducted at the MACV Recondo School, a special institution established in September 1966 largely to provide personnel for the Greek-letter projects.

One unit whose role fell between the special operations carried out by indigenous personnel and the CIDG Program was the 'Apache Force'. This interesting unit was made up of Montagnard CIDG troops and Special Forces advisers who specialised in orientating newly arrived US ground troops for operations in Vietnam. After it had prepared the men for battle and warned them against the booby traps and other weapons employed by the VC, the Apache Force would usually accompany them on operations for their first few days in the combat zone. Later, the Apache Force evolved into the combat reconnaissance platoons which played such an important part in the Mike Force attacks that characterised the later aggressive CIDG strategy.

Above: Robert Chestnut of the 5th Special Forces Group (left foreground) advises a CIDG commander (right foreground) on the deployment of his troops, during an operation near the Cambodian border.

By 1967, the CIDG camps were being constructed as 'fighting camps' designed to withstand heavy enemy attack through deep pre-planned defences, and machine guns and mortars in interlocking fields of fire. The CIDGs also intensified their night operations during this period and there was a marked rise in VC casualties. By 1967 the LLDB was also showing some improvement, partly as a result of US Special Forces Detachment B-51 at Dong Ba Thin. This improvement in the LLDB began to make it feasible for the US Special Forces to hand over control of a number of CIDG camps to the South Vietnamese, an expedient which had not been implemented since the Montagnard rebellion of 1964.

## Irregulars played a large part in clearing the VC from the Plain of Reeds

Forward planning for the CIDGs in 1967 and 1968 saw overall emphasis remaining on the construction of CIDG border surveillance camps to interdict VC infiltration routes. In the Mekong Delta, where Special Forces-trained irregulars had played a large part in clearing the VC from the Plain of Reeds, Special Forces bases were built as floating camps. Landing pads, barracks and store-rooms were built on platforms that rose with the river waters, thus allowing the camps to remain in operation when the delta was flooded. The Mike Force attached to IV Corps, which operated in the delta, was equipped with air boats and hydrofoils.

## MIKE FORCES

As the CIDG Program expanded, cutting into Viet Cong communications and negating communist influence in the Highlands, the CIDG camps came under increasingly concentrated attack. In response, the formation of Mobile Strike Forces (Mike Forces) was authorised in October 1964, and operations began in mid-1965. Originally totalling 600 men, the forces were organised into units of three companies and a headquarters.

Trained for airborne or airmobile warfare, Mike Forces comprised the elite, quick-reaction element of the CIDG camps. Unlike other parts of the CIDG organisation, they were exclusively controlled by the US Army Special Forces. Among the early Mike Force recruits were many members of the ethnic Chinese Nung tribe.

So successful was the Mike Force concept that by July 1968 11,000 men were involved, with 34 companies distributed between five Mobile Strike Force Commands (MSFCs). Of these commands, 5th MSFC came directly under the 5th Special Forces Group (Airborne), while the 1st to the 4th MSFCs were attached to I, II, III and IV Corps Tactical Zones of the US Army in Vietnam. Each MSFC had its own fixed number of battalions, depending on operational necessity, plus a reconnaissance company and a headquarters. The 4th MSFC also maintained an assault boat company. By the autumn of 1968 5th Special Forces Group was employing 3500 men, supervising 7000 Mike Force personnel and 27,000 CIDG.

The 1st Mobile Strike Force Command was based at Da Nang, 2nd at Pleiku, 3rd at Long Hai and 4th at Can Tho; based at Nha Trang, the 5th MSFC was deployed all over Vietnam.

# War in the Hills

Right: A captain of the Camp Strike Force, 5th Special Forces Group in Vietnam during 1965. This officer, working on the Montagnard CIDG Program, is dressed in green jungle fatigues with black leather and nylon boots. Rank is denoted by the silver bars on the beret badge and the white lapel bars. The breast wings indicate that this Green Beret is paratrained and he also wears the artillery badge – crossed guns and missile. Armament consists of an M2 carbine and a .45in calibre Colt M1911A1 pistol attached to M56 webbing.

Early in 1967, CIDG units began operations from camps opened in War Zone C, for years a notorious VC stronghold. Other hard-contested areas also came under CIDG control as strategic military bases were established. These camps came under constant attack by the Viet Cong and by the North Vietnamese Army (NVA), and were successfully defended only by deployment of Mike Forces in conjunction with US gunships such as the AC-47 (known as 'Puff the Magic Dragon'). During this period the Mike Forces were organised into companies of three rifle platoons and a weapons platoon, a total of 185 men. Though lightly equipped, the Mike Forces could bring devastating firepower to bear by calling down air strikes or artillery support.

Left: Captain Roger Donlon, who led the defence of Nam Dong in July 1964, for which he was awarded the Medal of Honor. Below: Donlon in the camp at Nam Dong after the VC attack.

## DEFENCE OF NAM DONG

In July 1964 the remote CIDG camp of Nam Dong, 15 miles from the Laotian border and surrounded by 2000ft mountains, was scheduled to be handed over to the Vietnamese Civil Guard. The camp's Special Forces A-Team, A-726, was led by Captain Roger H. C. Donlon. Then, at 0230 hours on the 6th, Viet Cong white phosphorus shells and grenades began to rain down onto the buildings – about 900 Viet Cong guerrillas had massed to destroy the camp.

Before long the entire camp was ablaze, with men running desperately to collect guns and ammunition from the burning huts. Following an urgent call for help, the radio shack was destroyed. After 15 minutes the Viet Cong appeared at the perimeter to finish off the garrison. Wounded in the stomach, Donlon killed a 3-man demolition team at the gate, all the time directing his men's fire and attempting to help casualties. At 0404 hours a flare-ship from Da Nang arrived to bathe the scene in an eerie light. Calls from the Viet Cong for surrender were answered with a hail of fire and eventually the Viet Cong, aware that reinforcements were imminent, began to withdraw. In the camp, 55 men lay dead, and another 65 were wounded. For his courageous leadership in the defence of Nam Dong, Captain Donlon received the Medal of Honor.

The CIDG Program benefited greatly from its logistical organisation, one which effectively circumvented both the corrupt South Vietnamese system and the cumbersome arrangements of the US Army. The CIDG Program and other Special Forces operations were supplied from forward bases in each of the four Corps Tactical Zones. Fighting camps could be re-supplied very quickly, using aerial re-supply if necessary. Any special items, such as long-range patrol rations specifically designed for the diets of indigenous troops, were acquired through the US Army Counter-Insurgency Support Office at Okinawa. The Special Forces supply network also provided special equipment such as foreign weapons for clandestine operations.

## During the Tet Offensive the cidgees gained respect as urban fighters

When the Tet Offensive descended on the populated areas of South Vietnam in January 1968 the cidgees gained a great deal of respect as urban fighters. Indeed, they inflicted a severe blow to VC morale after some attackers launched their part of the offensive prematurely against cities, such as Ban Me Thuot and Nha Trang, garrisoned by Mike Forces. Not only were the US units alerted to the offensive by these ill-coordinated attacks, but the raiders were also driven back by the Special Forces-trained Montagnards.

During the build-up for the Tet Offensive, and in the course of the offensive itself, most of the CIDG camps

Top: Training cidgees in the use of the M79 grenade launcher. Throwing a grenade to a maximum range of 400m, the M79 was a significant improvement to the close-quarters firepower of an infantry squad.

other than those of I Corps were left alone as VC strength concentrated near the cities. However, as VC and NVA elements massed around Khe Sanh and the northern cities such as Hue, Special Forces camps, such as Lang Vei, under I Corps' Special Forces Detachment A-101, came under heavy fire. Lang Vei had been attacked frequently since its establishment in December 1966, and on 4 May 1967 it had been virtually destroyed in an assault which included VC infiltrators within the ranks of the camp's own Montagnards. Lang Vei was finally overrun during the Tet Offensive on 7 February 1968 by a tank-supported NVA force.

After distinguishing themselves in the Tet Offensive the cidgees enjoyed a greater respect within the framework of the anti-communist forces. They were subsequently deployed in the defence of II, III, and IV Corps, while conventional units of the Army of the Republic of Vietnam (ARVN) were moved into I Corps to win back areas newly occupied

Below: Willie C. Smith of the 1st Special Forces Group trains Vietnamese troops in the use of hand grenades, at the Nui Ba Den outpost.

Below: Smith and his trainees cautiously watch the effects of the grenade burst. Nerve and skill are needed to use grenades properly.

Above: Cidgees help a wounded comrade back to base after an engagement with communist forces.

Below: Two members of the Special Forces relax prior to an operation in War Zone C, northwest of Saigon. They are armed with CAR-15 Colt Commandos (one fitted with a grenade launcher), and an M3A1 sub-machine gun.

by the North Vietnamese. CIDG units were also given priority in weapons re-supply, and they received issue of M16 rifles and M60 GPMGs in April 1968.

Beginning early in 1968, the process of turning over CIDG camps to Vietnamese control was speeded up. As the mission of countering infiltration assumed even more importance in the aftermath of the Tet Offensive, CIDG personnel were used primarily along the western border of South Vietnam to interdict infiltration routes. More and more responsibility for the CIDG Program, however, was being turned over to the LLDB to prepare them for the complete absorption of the programme. Special Forces civic action and psychological operations (psyops) were also turned over to the Vietnamese as rapidly as possible under the Nixon administration's policy of 'Vietnamization'.

## They assaulted a VC training area and uncovered large caches of weapons

Even though the directing of strategic border surveillance and interdiction camps was being turned over to the LLDB during 1969, Special Forces strength in Vietnam peaked in that year at over 4000 men, though some were assigned to special operations units and were thus only under 5th SFG (Airborne) control in theory. By early 1970, it had been decided to end the CIDG Program and absorb the CIDG units into the ARVN. A few camps were closed down during the autumn of 1970, but 37 were converted to ARVN Ranger camps with their CIDG complement becoming ARVN Ranger battalions, primarily 'Border Rangers' who retained the mission of countering infiltration along the borders.

During 1970, CIDG units participated in operations in Cambodia along with some Special Forces members. CIDG companies from Doc Hue and Tra Cu played an especially important role when they assaulted a VC training area and uncovered large caches of crew-served weapons and other equipment.

On 31 December 1970 the participation of the 5th SFG (Airborne) in the CIDG Program officially ended and on 3 March 1971 it officially departed for Fort Bragg, though some Special Forces troopers assigned to advisory missions or special operations were to remain in Vietnam much longer.

Overall, the CIDG Program was successful, the Mike Forces ranking among the best indigenous Vietnamese troops of the war. The CIDG Program, along with the heavy blow landed on the Viet Cong during the Tet Offensive, made a real contribution to containing communist insurgency in Vietnam. If there was one problem with the CIDG Program it was that the Special Forces performed the 'hearts and minds' aspect of their mission too well. The Nungs, Montagnards and other ethnic minorities readily gave their loyalty to the Special Forces, and, by association, to America, but never to the government of South Vietnam.

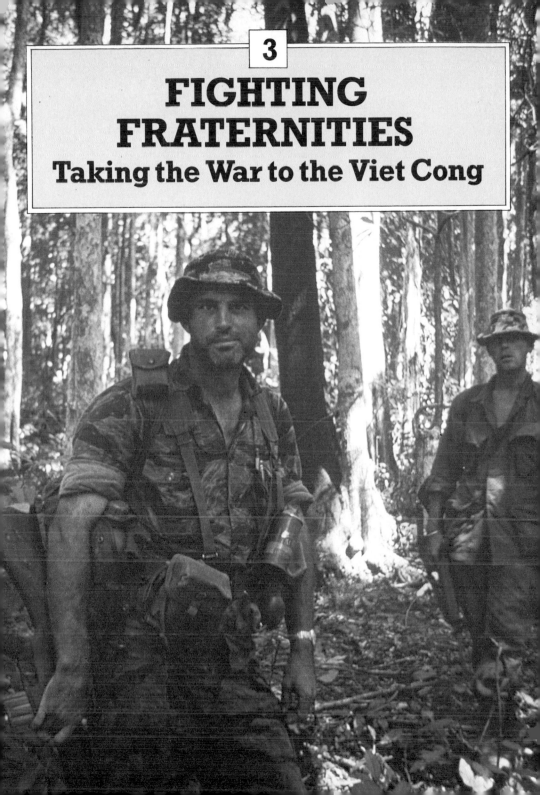

# 3

# FIGHTING FRATERNITIES
## Taking the War to the Viet Cong

Page 41: A Special Forces recon team in South Vietnam pauses for a moment.
Above: 'Bull' Simons, one of the best Special Forces officers.
Right: Taking the difficult way across a river – the VC laid booby traps at obvious crossing places.
Below: A US adviser watches operations in War Zone C.

SIX CLAYMORE mines erupted simultaneously across a 75yd section of jungle track. Those Viet Cong (VC) not killed outright hit the deck as a barrage of CAR-15 automatic fire and rounds fired from sawn-off M79 grenade launchers added to the cacophony of battle. Only one guerrilla survived the deadly storm, and, as he lay pressed to the cool jungle earth, a menacing, green-clad snatch squad, consisting of a Green Beret officer, a South Vietnamese officer, and an interpreter, raced across the track to corner their prey.

Dragging the prisoner to his feet, the squad headed for cover and began to move back to the pre-arranged rendezvous, their line of withdrawal covered by the other members of the 12-man recon team. To prevent an enemy follow-up, the two flank parties activated the 60-second delay fuzes on a

Above: South Vietnamese members of a recon team move cautiously out from the shelter of a river bank during a patrol.

pair of Claymores. Less than an hour later, the team was back at base, their captive handed over for interrogation.

The VC were learning that it was hard to hide from the recon teams, who would often appear from nowhere in the gloom of the South Vietnamese jungle to wreak havoc, and then fade back into the countryside, their mission accomplished. 'Sat Cong' (kill communists) was the motto of many recon teams.

The central coordinating body responsible for organising and evaluating the performance of field teams, was the Military Assistance Command Vietnam, Studies and Observations Group (MACV/SOG). More commonly known as the Special Operations Group, SOG was activated in 1964 and through MACV was directly accountable to the US Joint

## EXTRACTIONS

The rapid evacuation of a recon team from a combat zone was of paramount importance to the outcome of an intelligence mission. As with insertions, helicopters were usually used. Flying low and fast, pilots would drop into a landing zone at a steep angle to recover the team, the whole operation being completed in a matter of seconds.

On many occasions, however, it was impossible for the choppers to land due to enemy ground fire or the lack of a suitable clear site. Rope ladders proved the next most successful method of extraction. Dropped from a hovering aircraft, each ladder could support the weight of up to three team members at one time. The other means of extraction was by using a nylon webbing rig. Much like a simplified parachute harness, the wearer could, by attaching the rig to a rope hanging down from the helicopter, be drawn quickly aloft.

The existing McGuire rig, however, proved unsatisfactory, and staff members at the 5th SFG (Airborne) Recondo School designed an improved rig named STABO. This was easier to use and more reliable than its predecessor and even enabled team members to use their weapons while being extracted.

Chiefs of Staff through the Special Assistant for Counter-Insurgency and Special Activities.

Although the most widely known functions of Special Forces teams in Vietnam were training and advisory, the Green Berets were also heavily committed to several types of undercover operations, both within and far beyond the borders of South Vietnam. Many of these missions involved the collection of detailed and up-to-the-minute intelligence within enemy-controlled areas. However, Special Forces teams also had a much more aggressive role to perform. Assassination, sabotage, psychological warfare, snatches and rescue missions all fell within the scope of Special Forces 'black ops'.

When established, SOG was a joint-services outfit drawing on the cream of all four branches of the US armed forces. Some of the toughest, most resolute fighters available were recruited: Navy SEALs, Marine Recons, air jockeys from the 90th Special Operations Wing and, above all, members of the Green Berets. Highly-trained 'indigs' (indigenous personnel) from local tribes were also attracted to SOG. Crack helicopter crews were always available to insert and extract SOG teams in enemy territory, and certain naval craft were also on hand to carry out clandestine insertions into North Vietnam.

## The newly-created SOG attracted some of the finest senior officers available

The newly-created SOG also attracted some of the finest, most experienced senior officers available, such as Colonel John Singlaub and the redoubtable Brigadier-General Donald Blackburn, whose behind-the-lines experience in the Philippines during World War II was to prove invaluable. Another legendary Special Forces officer who served with Blackburn was 'Bull' Simons, who organised many of the covert operations into Laos, Cambodia and North Vietnam.

At its peak, SOG consisted of around 2000 US personnel and 8000 indigs. A percentage of the Americans in SOG were drawn from the 5th Special Forces Group (Airborne) – 5th SFG (Airborne) – who while in Vietnam were assigned to a shadowy organisation known as the Special Operations Augmentation. In practice, however, SOG also contained members of both the 1st and 7th SFG (Airborne), who carried out SOG missions while on six-month TDY (temporary duty) tours in-country.

SOG's headquarters was located close to Saigon near the town of Tan Son Nhut. Although particular missions were normally planned at this HQ, they were generally launched from forward sites originally called Forward Observation Bases (FOBs), but later known as Command and Control (CC) sites. Other types of special operations were carried out by Mobile Launch Teams from Ban Me Thuot, Kontum, Khe Sanh and Da Nang.

In November 1967, the coordination of SOG missions devolved to three CC units, each responsible for a particular combat zone. Command and Control North (CCN) was based at Da Nang to oversee missions into Laos and North Vietnam, Command and Control Central (CCC) was based at Kontum to carry out operations in the area where the borders of South Vietnam, Laos and Cambodia met, and the third body, Command and Control South (CCS), was based at Ban Me Thuot for operations into Cambodia.

The primary operational unit of each CC site was known as a Spike Recon Team, consisting of three Special Forces and nine indigs. Recon Teams (RTs) usually took their names from snakes or US states, such as RT Anaconda or RT Montana. At the peak period of SOG activity operational RTs numbered around 70. The RTs were backed up by Hatchet Forces which comprised five Special Forces personnel and up to 309 indigs. These teams were well-trained and experienced, specialists in ambushing enemy troops infiltrating into South Vietnam. RTs, however, were only the eyes and ears of the undercover forces, and it was the Hatchet Force

Below: Once the job was done, recon teams had to get away fast, and the best method was usually by helicopter.

Left: Guiding in a helicopter to evacuate a wounded team member. Effective care of injured personnel was one of the prime considerations of recon team leaders. Although Green Berets were trained to deal immediately with most injuries, severe wounds required the evacuation of the victim.

and the four SLAM (Search–Locate–Annihilate–Mission) companies that provided the cutting edge to their activities. Acting on information provided by the RTs, these rapid reaction forces were often inserted by helicopter to attack enemy bases or set up ambushes.

Often confused with SOG, but having a similar role, were the 'Greek-letter projects': Delta, Sigma, Omega and Gamma. These four projects grew out of Operation Leaping Lena in which US Special Forces personnel trained local troops to carry out long-range recon patrols. Leaping Lena evolved into the first and most famous Project – Delta.

During the early stages, only one Special Forces A-Team was attached to Delta, although by the early 1970s almost 1000 men were involved in operations. Unlike SOG, however, Project Delta drew most of its personnel from the 5th SFG (Airborne). Delta was organised into 12 tight-knit, highly skilled reconnaissance teams made up of two Green Berets and four indigs each. Delta also had six (later expanded to 12) Roadrunner teams, each consisting of four indigs, whose role was to move along the enemy's infiltration routes disguised as guerrillas, report back to base, and call up the 'killer' element of the project: a South Vietnamese Ranger battalion.

RECON INSIGNIA

Most recon teams in Vietnam were named after either a US state or snake and, although risking official censure, all had personalised badges made up by local tailors. Popular aggressive emblems included skulls, tigers, birds of prey and even alligators. Worn on the upper arm, the badges were worn not only as a means of identifying a particular unit, but also as a mark of their individuality.

The 281st Assault Helicopter Company provided Delta with its own lift capability.

When Project Delta began, the infiltration of recon and Roadrunner teams was effected by parachute, often at night, but helicopters and other means were also used later. Fighting or reconnoitring in the jungle was both time consuming and strength sapping, and it was vital that the teams were well-supplied with every type of combat necessity. To disguise the exact location of a team, elaborate deception measures were devised to mask the influx of supplies. Both

Below: Taking a captured Viet Cong officer back to Saigon for interrogation after a successful 'snatch' operation by a recon team.

Communication was vital to the success of the Greek letter projects. Equipment had to be in tip-top condition (far left, a communications supervisor of 5th Special Forces Group changes the crystals of a transceiver). When teams in the field could relay accurate information on the radio (left) then communist concentrations could be vigorously attacked by bombs and artillery (below).

Delta and SOG teams were often resupplied by dropping fake bombs or napalm canisters containing supplies and equipment in the vicinity of their area of operations.

Delta proved to be so successful that it was expanded to include over 1200 indigs, and three other projects, Sigma, Gamma and Omega, were activated in 1966 and 1967. Although the four projects concentrated on the unglamorous task of intelligence gathering, targets of opportunity were attacked if encountered.

Although the precise details of the missions undertaken by the various recon forces remain shrouded in official secrecy, certain aspects of their field procedures can be gleaned from available material.

Activated in 1964, Delta was a self-contained group specifically created to carry out hazardous intelligence gathering and hunter-killer missions against the communist forces operating in the South Vietnamese border areas. Unlike the other Greek-letter projects (Omega, Sigma and Gamma), Delta was run jointly by both US and South Vietnamese Special Forces. As the project grew in size and scope, Delta's operations were controlled by Detachment B-52.

Under B-52, Delta was organised into 12 (later 16) reconnaissance teams, each made up of two US Special Forces and four indigenous personnel. The other undercover teams within Delta were known as Roadrunners. Dressed as guerrillas, these groups comprised four locals and worked along known enemy infiltration routes.

Delta also had its own quick reaction force, the 91st Ranger Battalion (Airborne) of the South Vietnamese Army, which was flown into action by the 281st Assault Helicopter Company. When Delta reached full strength, the US Special Forces were working with nearly 1200 indigs, drawn from the Nung tribe. The other Greek-letter projects also included ethnic Cambodians, Chams and Montagnards.

Aside from the more warlike activities, Delta was also closely involved in the training of other recon teams at the Recondo School.

To carry out their highly dangerous missions, the various recon units were equipped with a variety of specialist weapons and equipment. Uniforms, for example, were never standardised; jungle fatigues, either dyed or splattered with black paint, were often worn both by the Special Forces and the indigs. Bandannas were used to cover the face and break up the tell-tale figure silhouette. Captured enemy clothing and equipment were also carried on operations to disguise a team's true identity. Frequently, USAF survival vests were worn, their pockets stuffed with a bewildering variety of essential escape and evasion aids.

Recon teams paid particular attention to their footwear. Jungle boots or 'Bata' sneakers were popular, and a type of shoe with rubber moulds of Vietnamese bare feet attached to the soles was experimented with but proved to be extremely uncomfortable and became little more than a novelty item. In fact, the footprints left by these shoes when worn by a Green Beret were so much larger and deeper than those left by a guerrilla that the enemy were rarely fooled.

## Many recons were hotly pursued by guerrillas as they withdrew

Other items of specialist equipment, however, were more realistic and of lasting value. STABO rigs, which allowed a team member to be extracted while still firing his weapon, were much prized, particularly as many recons were often hotly pursued by guerrillas as they withdrew. A few extractions were even made by skyhook, a device consisting of a large balloon and harness which could be snatched aloft by a low-flying aircraft.

Although recon teams often avoided 'live' contact with the enemy, many were walking arsenals. The most common sidearm was the handy Browning 9mm pistol or the .22in Ruger automatic with silencer, used to take care of VC sentries with the minimum of fuss. Larger weapons included the CAR-15 version of the M16, the Swedish K 9mm submachine gun and a variety of carbines. Additional weaponry might include a sawn-off M79 grenade launcher which, usually affixed to a team member's webbing and loaded with a canister round, could be used as a giant 'shotgun' to clear an enemy patrol from a trail.

Armed with this deadly array of ordnance, the various recon teams tended to follow a similar pattern when in the field. After arriving at an FOB, the RT commander, often a junior officer, would brief the local officers on the precise aims of his operation, the strength of his team, its area of operations and the methods of insertion and extraction.

Just before last light, the recon team would be assembled at the base landing zone to rendezvous with their helicopters – their weapons, radios and equipment checked and cleaned, their faces blacked up. Insertions at dusk were favoured as pilots were able to fly to the landing site and escape before the inky Vietnamese night shrouded both them and the recon team in its embrace.

Below: A recon team, its members festooned with the varied and deadly weaponry that they used against the communist forces.

On landing, the team leader would gather his men, take bearings and then plunge into the jungle. During movement to the objective, the team took great care to avoid VC booby traps, mines and punji stake traps. Stealth was vital: hand and arm signals were used instead of voice commands, radio messages were kept short and weapons were padded.

Sites for setting up camp or receiving supplies were always arranged and plotted before a mission. A team's main needs were for a site that was defensible, with good cover and ready access to water. However, as a recon was essentially aggressive, few teams ever occupied a bivouac for more than a few hours. Any longer, and the VC were likely to be snapping at the team's heels.

## The key part of any reconnaissance was gathering intelligence

The key part of any reconnaissance was gathering intelligence and every team member was fully trained in interpreting and reading the signs left by the enemy. Even the most seemingly inconsequential find might yield extremely valuable information. On one occasion a recon team discovered numerous piles of fresh elephant dung below a ridge line. Further investigation on the crest revealed recently abandoned gourds and small rifle pits. Piecing all the

Below: Vietnamese troops keep a look-out for enemy forces. Armed with an M2 carbine, the soldier in the foreground is carrying machine-gun ammunition.

At the heart of all Special Forces operations in Vietnam was the collection of accurate intelligence. Left: Green Berets Captain Myers and Lieutenant Deason (on right), together with South Vietnamese troops in tiger-stripe camouflage, question a village chief and his assistant.
Above right: Collating the information from captives and examining documents to build up a picture of enemy strength.

evidence together, it was estimated that a VC force of approximately battalion strength, using elephants for transportation, had occupied the site within the last 48 hours. From the direction of the tracks leading away from the position, the team was able to plot the route taken by the enemy. If the contact had been fresher, the team leader would have called in either a 'killer' force or an air strike against the unit.

Footprints were another valuable source of intelligence, and recons were taught to identify the number of people in an enemy patrol, the direction of movement, and even the type of load being carried. Under normal conditions, spaced footprints with unusually deep toe marks indicated that the person leaving the prints was carrying a heavy load. Team members were also trained to take into account the effects of wind, rain and sunlight on tracks.

If it became clear that a particular trail was in constant use, the recon team might lay an ambush or carry out a snatch to capture a guerrilla. To avoid getting involved in a firefight, teams often left the enemy a calling card: Claymore mines with a delay fuze, M14 mines planted in a triangular pattern across the track, or trip-wires attached to fragmentation grenades.

After completing an operation, the recon teams would rendezvous at a pre-arranged landing zone for extraction. Again, helicopters were the favoured method of departure from the patrol area. If time permitted, the pilots would bring their choppers in to land, but if the enemy was in hot pursuit of a team, other, faster methods such as the STABO rig would

Above: Waiting and watching, the recon and 'killer' teams took an undercover war to their communist opponents in the mountains, jungles and swamps of South Vietnam.

be used. Back at base, the team leader would be debriefed and the information collated and assessed.

Although the scale and frequency of recon and 'killer' missions in Vietnam varied from month to month, most units spent up to 60 per cent of their tours of duty in Vietnam on active operations.

Despite the frequent success of recon teams, they could never off-set the US armed forces' inability to come to grips with waging a war against an unconventional enemy, and as the American commitment in Vietnam was wound down, many of the Special Forces teams were deactivated. By the early 1970s, the four Greek-letter projects, arguably the finest realisation of the recon idea, had been disbanded, and the other long-range penetration units were being withdrawn. Nevertheless, the concept had proved a valuable part of the US counter-insurgency effort.

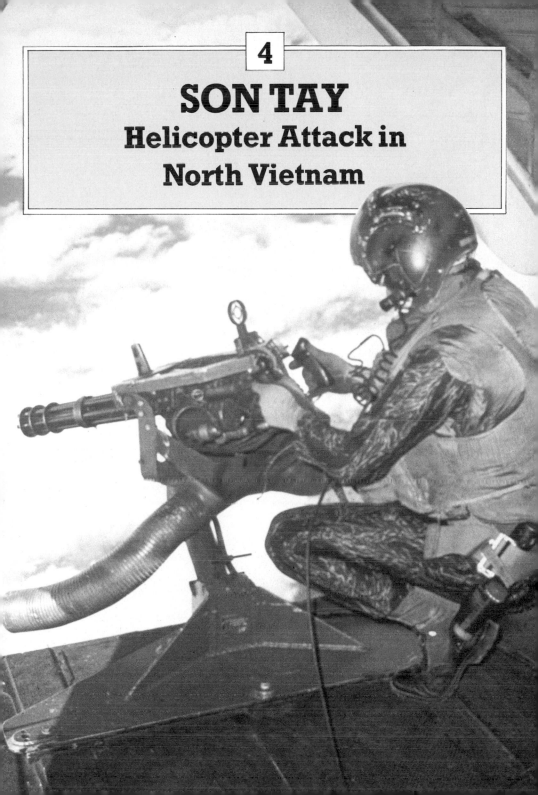

# 4

# SON TAY
## Helicopter Attack in
## North Vietnam

During the dozen years of direct US involvement in Vietnam some 800 Americans were held captive by the enemy. The majority of the prisoners were aircrew shot down during raids over North Vietnam.

The US POWs were placed in several camps scattered throughout the North, and their living conditions, although generally harsh, were survivable. The North Vietnamese held the view that the prisoners were not POWs but criminals and that their treatment was 'lenient and humane'.

Occasionally, some prisoners were released; for example, in the late 1960s, when three groups of three men were freed.

In 1970, US Special Forces launched the only attempt to free prisoners held in the North. Although the camp at Son Tay was empty, the raid forced Hanoi to improve the prisoners' conditions. After President Nixon's 1972 visits to China and the USSR, and the failure of the North's spring offensive, representatives of both sides met during the Paris peace talks and agreed a timetable for the repatriation of prisoners. The exchange of captives began in February 1973, just a month after the peace accords were signed. Over the next two months, some 600 US prisoners were released. It is known that over 70 Americans died in prison and that, although escape attempts were common, only 30 men successfully evaded their pursuers.

WHEN, ON 9 May 1970, an NCO of the USAF's 1127th Field Activities Group (1127th FAG), a special intelligence unit that correlated information about American POWs in North Vietnam, spotted what appeared to be a prison full of American POWs at Son Tay, some 23 miles west of Hanoi, from reconnaissance photographs, he started a chain of events that would eventually lead to one of the most daring Special Forces operations of the entire war. Once the Joint Chiefs of Staff had evaluated the information from the 1127th FAG and decided that a rescue was desirable, both for the well-being of the prisoners and for the morale of American fighting men and civilians, the go-ahead was given for SACSA (the Special Assistant for Counter-Insurgency and Special Activities), Brigadier General Donald Blackburn, to begin planning a rescue mission to free the Son Tay POWs.

Various photo-intelligence sources, including the Big Bird reconnaissance satellite, the SR-71 Blackbird and Buffalo Hunter reconnaissance drones were also made available to gather the information necessary for the raid. By 5 June, a full briefing had been given to the Joint Chiefs, and Blackburn had received permission to continue planning the raid. A little over a month later, on 10 July, the Joint Chiefs gave the go-ahead to begin implementing the plan.

Blackburn, a real fire-eater who had commanded Philippine guerrillas during World War II and the Special Operations Group in Vietnam, wanted to lead the raid himself, but because of his knowledge of sensitive intelligence matters he was precluded. Instead, the assignment went to Colonel 'Bull' Simons, a highly experienced Special Forces officer who had served under Blackburn and had a reputation for

Page 55: A helicopter crewman mans a 7.62mm minigun. Such weapons were used to blast away the defences during the Son Tay Raid.
Left above: The model of the camp built to facilitate training.
Left: One of the aerial photographs used in the planning of the raid.
Right: Colonel 'Bull' Simons, the experienced officer who was chosen to lead the raid.

# Son Tay
## US Special Forces, 21 November 1970

In the early morning of 21 November 1970 a crack assault group of US Special Forces staged a daring raid on a North Vietnamese POW camp only 23 miles from Hanoi. The American POWs they hoped to free had been moved out – but the raid was executed with verve and the force pulled out without suffering a single serious casualty.

**Key**

→ Son Tay assault force

• North Vietnamese POW camps

⌁ Assault force helicopter landing zones

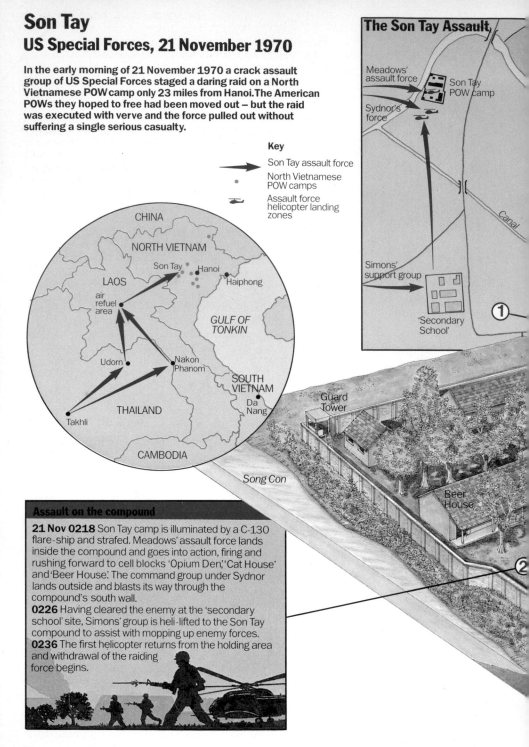

CHINA

NORTH VIETNAM

Son Tay · Hanoi

LAOS

air refuel area

Haiphong

*GULF OF TONKIN*

Udorn

Nakon Phanom

SOUTH VIETNAM

Da Nang

THAILAND

Takhli

CAMBODIA

### The Son Tay Assault

Meadows' assault force

Son Tay POW camp

Sydnor's force

Simons' support group

'Secondary School'

Canal

① 

Guard Tower

Song Con

Beer House

② 

### Assault on the compound

**21 Nov 0218** Son Tay camp is illuminated by a C-130 flare-ship and strafed. Meadows' assault force lands inside the compound and goes into action, firing and rushing forward to cell blocks 'Opium Den', 'Cat House' and 'Beer House'. The command group under Sydnor lands outside and blasts its way through the compound's south wall.

**0226** Having cleared the enemy at the 'secondary school' site, Simons' group is heli-lifted to the Son Tay compound to assist with mopping up enemy forces.

**0236** The first helicopter returns from the holding area and withdrawal of the raiding force begins.

getting things done. The raiding force was known as the Joint Contingency Task Group (JCTG), and the mission itself was code-named Ivory Coast. An area of Eglin Air Force Base in Florida was set aside for training the JCTG. Although Major-General Leroy Manor, the commander of USAF special operations at Eglin, was put in overall command, Simons was his deputy and in charge of leading the raiding force.

Since the optimum time for the raid appeared to be between 20 and 25 October, when the weather and moon would be most favourable, both men began selecting their teams: Manor, the air and planning elements, and Simons, the actual assault force. At Fort Bragg, hundreds of Special Forces troopers volunteered for the JCTG, knowing only that it was hazardous and that the 'Bull' would be commanding.

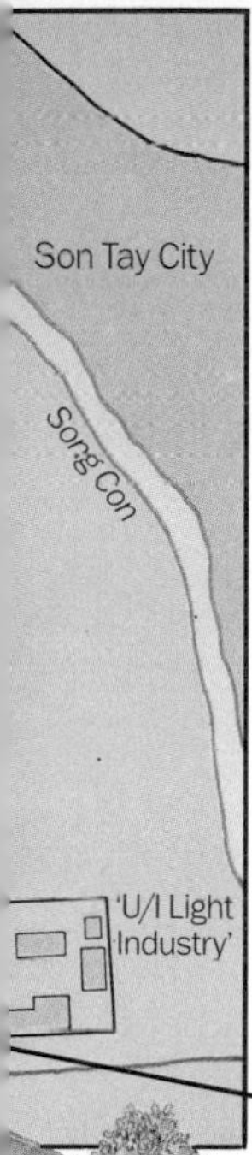

Son Tay City

Song Con

'U/I Light Industry'

## The Son Tay raiders

**18 Nov 0300** The Son Tay assault force arrives at Takhli air force base in Thailand. The order to go ahead with the raid is given.

**20 Nov** The raiders transfer to Udorn air force base.

**2318** The Son Tay raid is launched as the HH-53 helicopters and C-130 tankers leave Udorn.

**21 Nov** A-1 attack aircraft and a C-130 Combat Talon guide-plane leave Nakon Phanom and US Navy aircraft are launched from the Gulf of Tonkin to begin diversionary raids.

**0218** (Son Tay time) An HH-53 gunship helicopter strafes the guard tower of the Son Tay compound. As the assault group goes in, Simons' support force lands 400m to the south at a military installation mis-identified as a 'secondary school.'

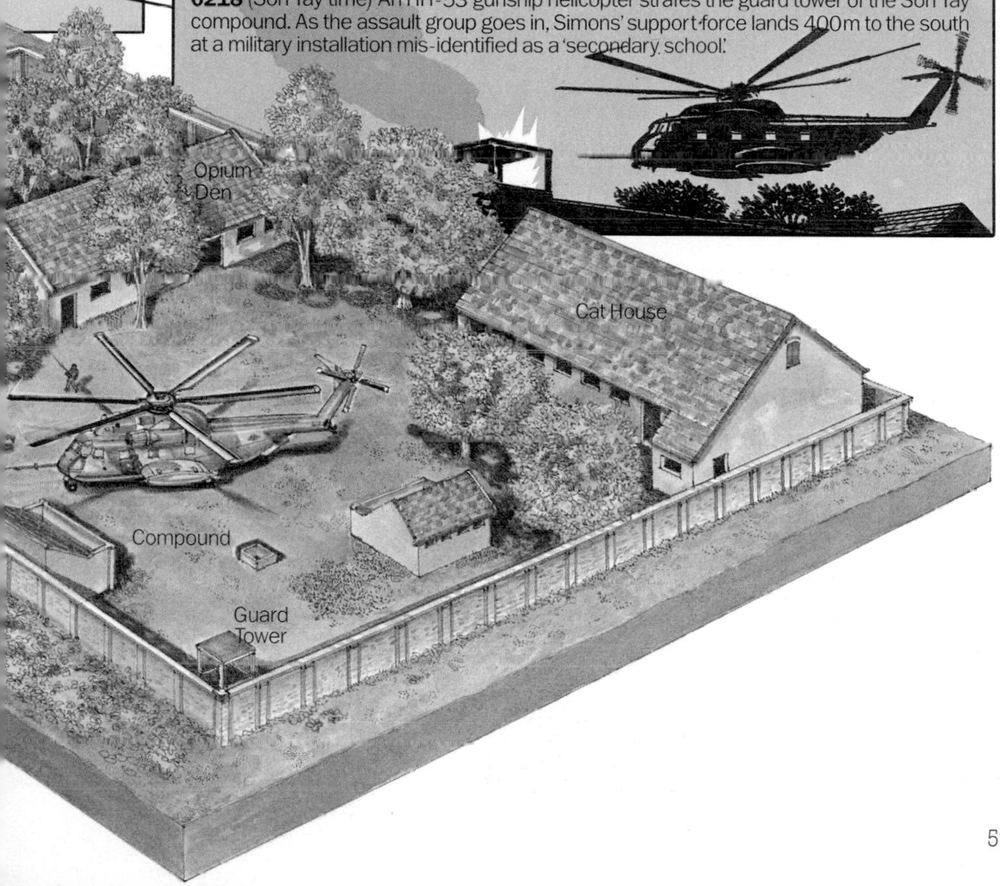

Opium Den

Cat House

Compound

Guard Tower

## TRANSPORT

The Special Forces deployed two types of helicopter in the Son Tay raid: the HH-53 Super Jolly Green Giant, and the HH-3 Jolly Green Giant.

Built by Sikorsky, the HH-53 was designed as a heavy assault transport helicopter and when the machine entered service in late 1967 it was the fastest and most powerful helicopter in the USAF. Despite a maximum weight of 42,000lb when fully loaded with either 37 troops or 24 litters and four attendants, the HH-53 has a range of 540 miles when fitted with auxiliary fuel tanks, and a speed of 186mph at sea level. During the attempt to free the prisoners, Super Jolly Green Giants were used in a fire-suppression role to take out enemy guard towers around Son Tay prison's perimeter wall. The HH-53s were fitted with three 7.62mm miniguns each.

Like the HH-53, the Jolly Green Giant was also designed by Sikorsky. A twin-engined all-weather search and rescue helicopter, the HH-3's first flight took place in 1963. Fully loaded, with a crew of four and up to 30 troops or 5000lb of cargo, the HH-3 has a maximum range of around 620 miles. Operating from Udorn in Thailand or out of Da Nang in South Vietnam, the Jolly Green Giant was capable of reaching any part of the North and making the return journey.

Above: During the Son Tay raid, the assault force helicopter men refuelled in the air on the journey to the objective. Here, an HC-130P version of the Hercules refuels an HH-53 Super Jolly Green Giant.
Right: Rappeling from a helicopter. Effective use of helicopters was the key to the Son Tay raid.
Below: Three participants in the raid pose for the camera on their return.

Some 15 officers and 82 NCOs, predominantly from the 6th and 7th SFG (Airborne), were chosen. As training progressed, the assault force, their back-ups, and the support personnel would be selected from these 97 Green Berets.

To carry out realistic training, a mock-up of the Son Tay compound was built at Eglin. So that Soviet spy satellites could not detect its presence, the mock-up was designed to be dismantled during the day and quickly set up at night for training. Since the raid itself would be at night, training at night on the mock-up was essential. As an additional training aid, a table-top model of the camp, costing some 60,000 dollars, was also built.

## Special night-sights were acquired for the sharpshooters' M16s

Detailed training of the raiding force began on 9 September. Two problems involving the elimination of guards at the prison arose during this period. Simons was dismayed to find that even his best marksmen were having trouble getting more than 25 per cent of their shots on target at night. This difficulty was solved, however, by going outside the normal army supply channels to acquire 'Singlepoint Nite Sites' for the sharpshooters' M16s. The other problem involved the need to saturate the guard towers around the Son Tay compound with fire. To solve this problem an HH-53 Super Jolly Green Giant equipped with 7.62mm miniguns was assigned to chopping the towers down with a hail of fire.

The assault force was formed into three groups: the compound assault force of 14 men, who would actually be deposited inside the prison compound by crash landing an HH-3 helicopter; the command and security group of 20 men; and the support group of 22 men commanded by Simons himself. Five HH-53s, which could be refuelled in-flight, and the HH-3 would carry the assault force.

Beginning on 28 September, the assault force practised the actual assault with the air force crews who would fly the helicopters and other aircraft, which included three C-130s (two of which were Combat Talons equipped for command and control) and A-1 strike aircraft. The landing and assault were rehearsed again and again, with many simulations being 'live-fire' run-throughs. Alternative plans were also produced in case one of the three teams failed to make it to the target.

As the rehearsals progressed, Simons, a firearms enthusiast and expert, ordered his supply people to come up with additional weapons and special equipment. Eventually, the teams were equipped with 12-gauge shotguns, 30-round M16 magazines, .45in automatic pistols, CAR-15s for the compound assault force, M79 grenade launchers, LAWs, bolt cutters, cutting torches, chainsaws, and special goggles. Some men carried cameras to record the prisoners' living conditions. Many items used in the raid had to be acquired outside the normal army supply channels. To ensure communications during those critical minutes on the

ground, the 56 men of Simons' assault force were given 92
radios: two AN-PRC-41s to maintain contact with the Pentagon via a radio link at Monkey Mountain in South Vietnam, 10
AN-PRC-77s for calling in air strikes, 24 AN-PRC-88s for
communications between the various groups on the ground,
and, finally, 56 AN-PRC-90 survival radios for escape and
evasion.

Above: The view from a Hercules
as a Super Jolly Green Giant is
about to link up for refuelling.
Above right: 'Bull' Simons explains
the details of the raid to pressmen,
using the model to describe the
various phases.

## The weather and moon had to be right for the raid to take place

Although the mission had not been approved by the target
date, Blackburn got the go-ahead to begin moving personnel to Southeast Asia in preparation for the mission on 27
October. On 1 November, Blackburn and Simons, among
others, left for Southeast Asia to lay the groundwork for the
raid. By the 12th, both Blackburn and Simons were back in
the States as the raiding force prepared to head for Thailand.
Six days later, a few hours after the raiders had left for Takhli
RTAFB (Royal Thai Air Force Base) in anticipation of receiving orders to carry out the raid, President Nixon gave the 'go'
order. The weather and moon had to be right for the raid to
take place and conditions were deemed acceptable on the
night of 20/21 November.

On the evening of 20 November, the raiders were shuttled
to Udorn RTAFB, from where the raid was launched at 2318
hours local time. Carrier aircraft from the *Oriskany*, *Ranger*
and *Hancock* were also launched a couple of hours later,
during the early morning of the 21st, to create a diversion by
staging a fake raid over Hanoi. At about 0218 on the morning
of 21 November, the raid itself began. As a C-130 flare ship
illuminated the area, the HH-53, code-named Apple Three,
opened up on the guard towers of Son Tay Prison with its
miniguns, bringing them crashing down.

Shortly afterwards, the HH-3 carrying the assault party, commanded by Major 'Dick' Meadows, landed inside the prison compound, the whole group pressed against mattresses to cushion them from the crash. The HH-3, known as 'Banana One', came to rest amid branches, leaves, and other debris brought down by its whirling rotors during the crash descent. On landing, 'Dick' Meadows rushed out with his bullhorn shouting: 'We're Americans. Keep your heads down. We're Americans. This is a rescue. We're here to get you out. Keep your heads down. Get on the floor. We'll be in your cells in a minute.' The remainder of the assault party rushed into action; some men laying down suppressive fire; others streaking for the cellblocks to rescue the prisoners.

## Within minutes many of the residents of the barracks had been killed

A few minutes later the command and security group landed just outside the prison walls. The support group led by Simons himself, however, had landed 400yd off course at what was identified on the raiders' maps as a secondary school. Instead of a secondary school, they found themselves outside a barracks housing Chinese or Soviet advisers to the NVA (North Vietnamese Army). School or not, Simons and his men proceeded to teach its denizens a lesson. Within minutes of touching down, many of the residents of the barracks had been killed, preventing them from reinforcing the prison compound and taking the other raiders by surprise. Within 10 minutes Simons had cleared the area and his men had been lifted back to the Son Tay compound,

Above: Brigadier-General Donald Blackburn, who headed the study team that developed the plan for the Special Forces raid on Son Tay.

Above: The unofficial badge that the Green Berets designed for themselves in connection with the Son Tay raid. The initials stand for: Kept In the Dark/Fed on Horse Shit, and the emblem is a stinking mushroom grown in a cellar. The Green Berets were infuriated that faulty intelligence had made their raid unnecessary and this badge reflected their anger.

where they assisted the assault and security elements in eliminating several guards.

Despite the smoothness of the assault, however, the raiders discovered that there were no POWs in the prison. They had been moved elsewhere some weeks before the raid. This development had not been picked up by US intelligence, because no-one had wanted to risk putting in any agents on the ground, and too much reliance had been placed on photographic intelligence.

## Casualties were light; the raid itself had gone almost perfectly

Less than 30 minutes after the raid had started, the raiders were back on board their choppers and heading for Thailand. Casualties were light: only one raider had been wounded. The raid itself had gone almost perfectly. Even Simons' landing at the wrong complex was fortuitous as it allowed a surprise attack on an undetected enemy unit.

The raiders themselves had mixed reactions on the flight back to Thailand. They were disappointed that all of their training and effort had not resulted in the rescue of a single prisoner. However, they were also glad that they were all heading home, and justifiably proud of the precision with which the raid had been carried out.

The Son Tay raid was not a complete failure, despite the fact that no prisoners were rescued. It proved in very striking fashion that the North Vietnamese were vulnerable to attacks on installations close to home. As a result, the North Vietnamese had to tie down additional troops to guard sensitive areas, and they also lost some credibility with the Chinese and Russians, who feared that the US would continue to mount raids into North Vietnam. Indirectly, the raid also led to some improvement in the treatment of American POWs.

It should not be forgotten, either, that Simons' party had killed dozens of the enemy, many of them foreign advisers, without taking any losses themselves. The Special Forces troopers and the air force and navy pilots had carried out their jobs with great skill. It was a classic raid – get in quick, hit hard, inflict maximum casualties, get out fast – but the intelligence had been wrong, a failure which clearly illustrated the fact that intelligence is critical to special operations, especially raids into enemy territory. It is still not known why the North Vietnamese moved their prisoners from Son Tay, but it may be speculated that a rescue attempt was foreseen as the US steadily built up pressure for the POWs' release.

The final point proven by the Son Tay raid was one that Donald Blackburn had been making ever since being appointed SACSA. He argued that North Vietnam was vulnerable to hit-and-run raids by highly-trained special operations forces. Other such raids might have secured the release of many of the American POWs held by the Hanoi government.

# 5

# PROTECTING THE BACKYARD
## Special Forces in Latin America

BY THEIR VERY nature, the peacetime activities of the US Special Forces tend to be conducted under a cloak of secrecy. They thus frequently pass unobserved, and even when they are noticed, the identification of the specific units involved varies from the difficult to the impossible. It is known, however, that elements of the Special Forces have been active continuously in various parts of Latin America since the early 1960s, either in direct military operations, usually of a counter-insurgency type, or in training local forces for this role. With the present state of political turmoil, particularly in Central America and the Caribbean, such activities may be expected to increase.

The triumph of the Cuban Revolution in 1959 and the subsequent Cuban attempts to export revolution throughout Latin America concentrated US attention on an area which it had long regarded as its exclusive sphere of influence. In 1961 the 7th Special Forces Group (Airborne) – a new, redesignated unit formed from the 77th SFG (Airborne) on 20 May 1960 – began conducting advisory missions in those Latin American countries considered to be most under threat of communist subversion. Company D of the 7th SFG (Airborne) was moved to Fort Gulick in the Panama Canal Zone the following year, where it formed the nucleus of the 8th SFG (Airborne) which was activated on 1 April 1962.

Fort Gulick was the location of the US Army Caribbean School, which had been established in 1949, mainly for the training of Latin American military personnel in advanced military technology. From 1956 onwards Spanish had replaced English as the teaching language, and in 1963 the title was changed to United States Army School of the Americas,

Previous page: A Green Beret, armed with a revolver, covers a doorway during a training exercise.
Above: A US military adviser helps a Salvadorean soldier during rifle training. Special Forces personnel trained Salvadorean units and participated in their operations from 1982 to 1984.

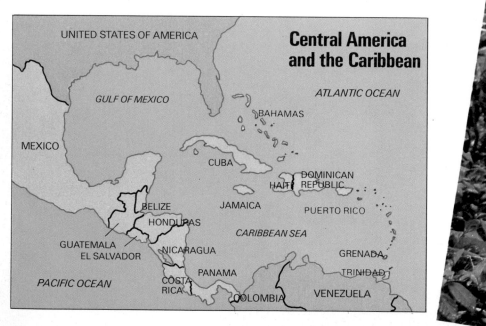

UNITED STATES OF AMERICA

**Central America and the Caribbean**

GULF OF MEXICO

ATLANTIC OCEAN

BAHAMAS

MEXICO

CUBA

DOMINICAN
HAITI REPUBLIC

BELIZE

JAMAICA

PUERTO RICO

HONDURAS

CARIBBEAN SEA

GUATEMALA
EL SALVADOR

NICARAGUA

GRENADA

PANAMA

TRINIDAD

PACIFIC OCEAN

COSTA
RICA

COLOMBIA

VENEZUELA

the emphasis in training becoming heavily orientated towards counter-insurgency techniques, under the tutelage of members of the 8th SFG (Airborne). By 1 October 1984, when Fort Gulick reverted to Panamanian control under the Panama Canal Treaty, over 44,000 Latin American military personnel had undergone counter-insurgency courses at the School.

## Bolivia and Guatemala were singled out by Cuban agitators

In addition to the training at the School of the Americas, the various US military missions which operated in all Latin American countries (following the ratification of the Rio Treaty of Reciprocal Assistance in 1947) were active in the formation of local special forces units. The first of these had been formed in Colombia as far back as 1955, and two existing infantry battalions of the Peruvian Army had been converted into commando units, with US assistance, during the early 1960s. From the mid 1960s Latin American governments were actively encouraged to establish specialist counter-insurgency forces. With training assistance from the US, Chile established a paratroop/special forces battalion in 1965, the Dominican Republic raised an airborne group of special forces within the Base Defence Command of its air force in 1966, and Colombia converted an existing paratroop battalion to an airborne special forces unit in 1968–69. Also with US assistance, Venezuela established no less than 13 rifle battalions with a specific counter-insurgency function during this period.

Below: Much of the terrain of Central America is covered by tropical rainforest. Here, at the School of the Americas in Panama, men are taught how to lay a trap for a large animal as part of a survival course.
Below right: Salvadorean officer-candidates scramble over an obstacle during their training.

The United States has been the strongest state in the western hemisphere since its independence in 1783. And when the former Spanish and Portuguese colonies of Latin America won their freedom in the early 19th century, they naturally looked to the United States for help to maintain their liberty. In 1823, the US pronounced the Monroe Doctrine, a somewhat grandiose proclamation insisting that any European involvement in the western hemisphere would be deemed a threat to the security of the United States, and this became a convenient justification for US intervention in Latin American affairs during the early part of the 20th century. These interventions reached their height during the 1920s, when US troops were deployed to Cuba, Nicaragua, the Dominican Republic and Haiti. The Roosevelt administration of the 1930s was more reluctant to use US troops to interfere in the affairs of its southern neighbours, and instead relied on local leaders to maintain US interests in Latin America. This remained US policy – with the notable exception of the intervention in the Dominican Republic in 1964 – until the Reagan administration's intervention in Grenada in 1983.

US Special Forces were also directly active in counter-insurgency operations in Bolivia and Guatemala between 1964 and 1968. Both of these countries had been singled out for particular attention by Cuban agitators on the basis that their large, downtrodden Indian majorities were considered to be ripe for revolution. Although this premise proved false in both cases, both countries did suffer from chronic rural guerrilla activity during the late 1960s, the insurgency in Bolivia being led by Ernesto 'Che' Guevara, the No.3 man of the Cuban Revolution.

As the local armed forces were at first unable to deal effectively with the guerrilla threat, the main brunt of counter-insurgency operations in both countries fell on the US Special Forces units (in each case *ad hoc* teams from the 8th SFG (Airborne) in Panama), whose presence had been requested by the Bolivian and Guatemalan governments. Almost simultaneously the Guatemalan Army established a company of special forces which became operational on 12 May 1967, while the Bolivian Army raised three full Ranger battalions, one of which was responsible for the interception of Guevara's guerrilla band and the capture and execution of its leader on 8/9 October 1967.

## Detachments continued to be dispatched to Latin America

When the local forces had learned to deal with guerrilla insurgency, the direct involvement of US Special Forces, at least on a large scale and overt level, ceased in both Bolivia and Guatemala, although training assistance continued. The Guatemalan special forces unit was subsequently increased to a brigade-sized Group, while the Bolivian Rangers were consolidated into two two-battalion regiments. During this period the Bolivians also established a paratroop/special forces battalion as a demonstration unit for the Centre for the Instruction of Special Troops at Cochabamba which had been set up with US assistance.

The 8th SFG (Airborne) remained the Special Forces unit with special responsibility for operations in Latin America until its deactivation on 30 June 1972. Its functions were then undertaken by the newly created 3rd Battalion of the 7th SFG (Airborne) at Fort Bragg, from which frequent detachments continued to be dispatched to wherever necessary in Latin America. Other elements of the 7th SFG (Airborne) also served sporadically in various parts of Latin America.

The counter-insurgency training of the local Latin American armed forces continued. The 3rd Battalion of the 7th SFG (Airborne) carried out exercises with the local armed forces in both El Salvador and Honduras during 1973. The Salvadorean Army had by then formed two special forces companies and Honduras had organised a single company of special forces, officially designated as a squadron – both with US training assistance. The Panamanian National Guard also included a US-trained special forces unit which was nominally a company but approached battalion strength.

From 1979 onwards Central America became a cockpit subsequently to be defined by President Reagan as the main battleground between democracy and communism. Chronic low-level insurgency had continued in Guatemala since the 1960s although Israel had taken over from the US as the major supplier of military training and equipment to the Guatemalan government during the Carter administration (1977–81). The triumph of the left-wing Sandinista Revolution in Nicaragua in July 1979 coincided with an escalation of the chronic insurgency in El Salvador to the level of a full-scale civil war.

Within weeks of the assumption of the US Presidency by Ronald Reagan on 20 January 1981, the US military mission in El Salvador was increased from 19 to 45 members. They were joined in March of the same year by 18 members of the

The outbreak of full-scale guerrilla warfare from the end of 1978 in El Salvador led to the training of three counter-insurgency battalions by US Forces, including the Green Berets (above left and above). The Atlacatl Battalion (below) is considered the finest of these units, and entered service in 1981.

## CUBA AND CASTRO

In 1952 Fulgencio Batista took power in Cuba in a coup and established a corrupt regime with the support of money from, among other sources, the Mafia in the United States. Opposition to his rule soon formed, and one of its leaders was a young lawyer, Fidel Castro. Castro supported a policy of revolutionary action against Batista. From 1953 onwards he organised insurrections against Batista, and from 1956 led a guerrilla army that had achieved total victory by January 1959.

Once in power, Castro attempted initially to follow a non-aligned foreign policy, but nationalised most US assets in Cuba. The US response was to sever relations with the Castro regime and impose economic sanctions. There were also attempts by the Central Intelligence Agency to overthrow the new Cuban government (the Bay of Pigs invasion in 1961) and to assassinate Castro himself. These attempts failed, and Castro became more closely aligned with the Soviet Union. The Cuban missile crisis of 1962 led to further animosity between the United States and Cuba, and Castro by now was lending strong support to revolutionary movements throughout Latin America. Cuba was openly attempting to export revolution, and was an enthusiastic backer of any anti-US forces. Not until 1979, however, did another revolutionary regime emerge – this time in Nicaragua. As in the early 1960s, this led to renewed US fears for the safety of its 'backyard' and heightened tension in the region.

1st Battalion of the 7th SFG (Airborne) who by April 1982 had trained the first of three Immediate Reaction Battalions of the Salvadorean Army. A total of 14 counter-insurgency rifle battalions (of the type established by the Venezuelan government with US assistance during the 1960s) was also subsequently raised by the Salvadorean Army. At the same time SEAL (Sea, Air, Land) commando instructors of the US naval mission established a small Salvadorean Marine Corps with a specific orientation towards counter-insurgency operations.

The US Special Forces instructors participated in operations with the Salvadorean forces from the outset. Such participation was consistently denied officially until the closing weeks of 1984, when it was simultaneously announced that the strength of the US military mission in El Salvador was being doubled and that the embargo on the participation of US military personnel in operations was being removed.

## The US military presence in Honduras was by now neither limited nor low-key

Following the accession of Ronald Reagan to the Presidency, military assistance to Guatemala, which had been suspended by President Carter due to that country's abysmal human rights record, was resumed, together with some covert assistance in counter-insurgency by Special Forces personnel. Israel, however, continued to be the main supplier both of equipment and training assistance. The US military presence in neighbouring Honduras was by now neither limited nor low-key. In addition to a permanent US military presence of about 1400 conventional forces, and a floating population which varied between 5000 and 30,000 engaged in a series of consecutive military exercises, Special Forces now became extremely active in that country.

On 17 May 1983, 200 members of the 3rd Battalion of the 7th SFGA arrived in Honduras and started to improve the counter-insurgency capabilities of the Honduran Army. They expanded the existing paratroop/special forces unit from squadron to battalion strength, and engaged directly in operations near the Salvadorean frontier.

With the running-down of the Panama Canal Zone as the main US military base in Central America, Honduras appears to have been selected as an alternative. Although no alternative location for the School of the Americas (following the takeover of its existing premises by Panama in October 1984) had been announced at the time of writing, its place had already largely been taken by the Region Military Training and Security Center which was set up at Puerto Castilla on the Caribbean coast of Honduras on 14 June 1983. By mid-1984 126 members of the 1st Battalion of the 7th SFGA had already trained some 8600 Honduran and Salvadorean military personnel in counter-insurgency techniques at Puerto Castilla.

The major recent overt involvement of US Special Forces in Latin America occurred with the Grenada operation of October 1983. Involved in this were the Delta Force (Special Operations Detachment Delta) and the 1st and 2nd Battalions of the 75th (Ranger) Infantry Regiment, together with elements of the 90th Civil Affairs Battalion and the 4th Psychological Operations Group – all of which form part of the US Army's 1st Special Operations Command – plus units of naval SEAL commandos.

In the Grenada invasion, titled Operation Urgent Fury, naval SEAL commando teams checked the beaches and harbours for obstacles and mines before two SEAL teams seized the transmitters of, respectively, Radio Grenada and the Governor's residence, during the early hours of 25 October 1983. The two Ranger battalions spearheaded the main assault, making a low-level parachute drop on Point Salines airfield which they secured after two hours of hard fighting against the mainly Cuban defenders. The safety of the students and faculty of the US-owned St George's Medical College had provided the main reason for the invasion, and less than two hours after the first troops had landed, the Rangers had secured this objective too. Meanwhile the SEAL commandos holding the Governor's residence had come under heavy pressure from Grenadan

Above: As well as military training, the Green Berets have also participated in medical assistance programmes.

71

Army units with armoured vehicle support, before being reinforced and ultimately relieved by a company of Marines during the late afternoon. The two Ranger battalions combined with the newly arrived Marine and paratroop units to make an assault on the Grande Anse medical school campus the following day; the campus was finally secured by Rangers airlifted in by Marine helicopters.

## Details of Delta Force activity in the Grenadan invasion remain shrouded in secrecy

The Marines and paratroops seem to have borne the brunt of the remainder of the fighting and the Rangers were airlifted back to their base at Fort Stewart, Georgia, on 28/29 October while mopping-up operations continued. The Civil Affairs and Psychological Operations units remained, and were active in the screening and political re-education of the Grenadan population after military operations ceased. Although elements of Delta Force are also known to have been present, their activities in the Grenada invasion remain shrouded in the secrecy associated with this unit.

As the precise extent of Special Forces activities in Latin America remains unknown it is difficult to arrive at an accurate assessment of their effectiveness. The earliest documented direct action of such forces was in Bolivia and

Above: Daniel Ortega Saavedra, co-ordinator of the junta established by the Sandinistas in Nicaragua in 1979.
Below: Members of ARDE (Alianza Revolucionaria Democrática), one of the groups fighting the Sandinista regime.

Guatemala during 1966-69. In both cases they performed what amounted to a holding action against active if limited guerrilla insurgency and appear to have been effective in its containment while local counter-insurgency forces were equipped and trained.

In Bolivia, the locally recruited but US-trained counter-insurgency forces were rapidly effective in not merely containing but virtually suppressing communist insurgency.

Top. Sandinista soldiers battle in a Nicaraguan town. The 1979 victory of the Sandinistas led to US fears that they supplied arms to the guerrillas in El Salvador. The Reagan administration involved Special Forces personnel in measures to support anti-Sandinista 'contra' groups engaged in military actions (such as the sabotage of oil storage tanks at Corinto, above; 1.5 million gallons of diesel were lost).

## SANDINISTAS VS CONTRAS

The opponents of the Sandinista regime in Nicaragua organised a counter-revolutionary force shortly after the overthrow of Anastasio Somoza in July 1979. They received some aid from Guatemala and set up a training camp there, and some also found a refuge in Honduras.

Shortly after they came to power, the Sandinistas began to strengthen their hold on the government, by excluding anti-Somoza elements unsympathetic to Sandinista dominance. The United States viewed this development with some alarm; the anti-American rhetoric of the Sandinistas did little to encourage US tolerance. The Reagan administration, which came to office in January 1981, began to give considerable aid to the two main groups of *contra-revolucionarios* ('contras'): the FDN (Fuerzas Democráticas Nicaragüenses – primarily made up of former National Guardsmen of the Somoza regime), and ARDE (the Alianza Revolucionaria Democrática – largely opponents of both Somoza and the Sandinistas).

Beginning in March 1982, the contras increased the level of their attacks, aiming at economic targets. The campaign was still continuing at the end of 1985. The United States has poured large amounts of aid into the contras' effort – approximately $20 million a year; in addition, the Central Intelligence Agency has given covert aid in the form of training and advice, and also operated support ships for raids on coastal installations. Soldiers who have received Special Forces training have been clandestinely involved too, as demonstrated by the deaths of two such persons, members of the Alabama National Guard, in a 1984 helicopter crash.

In Guatemala, although the locally raised forces kept the insurgency under control, they were unable to suppress it; indeed some of their own members, including several junior officers who had been trained at the School of the Americas, subsequently deserted to the guerrillas.

Likewise, in the current civil war in El Salvador, despite massive investment by the US in propping up the minority regime and a recent sensible trend towards supporting the moderate centre-right rather than the extreme reactionary element in Salvadorean politics, the US-trained and equipped armed forces – although increased in strength more

# Grenada
## US Airborne Forces, October 1983

On the morning of 25 October 1983 the United States launched Operation Urgent Fury with an airborne assault on the airstrip at Point Salines and a heliborne landing near Pearls airport. As a second Marine task force worked its way down from Grand Mal Bay, the airborne forces at Point Salines overcame Cuban and Grenadan resistance and pushed northwards. St George's fell late on 26 October and mopping up operations began.

Key — US forces

**Pearls and Grand Mal**

**25 Oct 0536** A Marine force seizes Pearls airport.
**1930** Marines land at Grand Mal Bay and advance towards St George's.

**St George's**

**25 Oct 0850** Rangers take True Blue Campus and release students.
**1400** 82nd Airborne Div arrives at Point Salines and relieves the Rangers there.
**26 Oct** The Rangers and 82nd Airborne advance northwards, taking Frequente and pushing on towards St George's.
**1600** Grand Anse Campus is secured and the students there are heli-lifted out. St George's falls after an airstrike.
**27 Oct** The remaining enemy positions are taken out and mopping up operations are under way.

**Point Salines**

**25 Oct 0530** One company of Rangers parachutes into Point Salines but is pinned down.
**0615** After Cuban defenders have been strafed by gunships, more Rangers drop into Point Salines and the airstrip is secured.

than sixfold – seem unable to maintain more than a precarious equilibrium with the less numerous and poorly equipped left-wing guerrillas.

Apart from Bolivia, the other major success in combating communist or other left-of-centre insurgency has been in Venezuela. Here, paradoxically, US training assistance concentrated on the creation of a relatively large number of medium-grade counter-insurgency troops rather than a smaller number of high-quality forces.

It appears that US elite forces are at best only equal in effectiveness in Latin America to the local forces they have trained. The level of success in suppressing armed insurgency is in the final analysis directly related to such primarily political factors as the presence or absence of extensive popular support for local guerrilla movements and the popularity or otherwise of the governments to which the US lends its support. Thus the successful ending of guerrilla insurgency in Bolivia and Venezuela owes at least as much to the apathy of the local population towards the aims of the guerrillas and the essentially democratic character of the supported government as it does to any purely military factor. The current situation in Central America faithfully

The most recent use of direct US military force in the Latin American/Caribbean region was the invasion of Grenada in October 1983. US forces (below, US Airborne troops on Point Salines airfield) faced the Grenadan Peoples' Revolutionary Army and Cuban workers with militia training, using Soviet-supplied equipment (right, BTR-60 APCs). Special Forces personnel from the Civil Affairs Battalion, the Psychological Operations Group and Delta Force were present on the island during the fighting. The Civil Affairs and Psychological Operations units remained after the rest of the US force had been withdrawn, to help ensure that the restoration of civil rule to Grenada would proceed smoothly.

mirrors that of Vietnam during the disastrous US involvement in that country. Although the US-trained counter-insurgency forces are militarily effective in the short term, the problem remains mainly a political one. A successful military solution depends ultimately on the installation of governments which can command popular support and erode support for the guerrillas.

The Grenada operation, which was the only instance to date in which US forces came into direct confrontation with Cuban- and Soviet-trained Latin American troops, leaves little room for US complacency. Here it took 18,000 US troops, most of them elite Rangers, Marines and paratroops, with massive naval and air support, four days to overcome a force of 2180 half-trained Grenadan troops, 784 Cubans (of whom only 36 were regular military personnel), and 96 assorted Eastern Europeans, Libyans and Koreans, equipped with only light infantry weapons, a few armoured personnel carriers, and without any artillery or air support whatsoever.

The primary role of special forces and the one in which they excel is the swift, decisive, limited operation, of which the Israeli raid on Entebbe in 1976, the British SAS involvement in the Iranian Embassy siege in 1980, the *Mayaguez* incident in 1975 and the French intervention in Kolwezi, Zaire, in 1978 are good examples. US experience in Latin America over the past 20 years shows that to involve such forces in a war of attrition, as is currently the case in Central America, can be tantamount to squandering a valuable and highly expensive asset.

Below: Jubilant medical students cheer the Rangers who seized the campus of St George's Medical College. The presence of these US citizens on Grenada was seen by President Reagan as a prime reason for the use of US troops on the island.

## 6

# EAGLE CLAW
## The Raid into Iran

Previous page: RH-53 Sea Stallions on board the USS *Nimitz* in the Persian Gulf.

Top left: The Sea Stallions take off for Desert One on 24 April 1980. They did not have sufficient range to fly from the *Nimitz* to Tehran, and thus were forced to make the fateful refuelling stop at Desert One.

Above left: The hostages from the US Embassy in Tehran were subjected to intense psychological pressure. Here one has been blindfolded and placed in front of television cameras amongst an anti-American crowd.

SHORTLY BEFORE 1800 hours on 24 April 1980, a lone MC-130E Hercules special operations transport thundered down the sun-baked runway at Masirah, an island off the coast of Oman, and rose gracefully into the darkening sky. Aboard, huddled shoulder to shoulder in the aircraft's cavernous cargo hold, their weapons secured to webbing above their heads, were members of the US Special Forces' Delta Force and their pugnacious commander, Colonel Charles Beckwith. After months of delay, uncertainty and detailed planning, Operation Eagle Claw, the daring bid to rescue 56 US nationals held in the Iranian capital of Tehran, was finally under way.

Delta Force, a branch of the Special Forces formed in 1978, had been intensively trained for just such a mission. The men were ruthlessly professional and highly motivated, yet they faced enormous, almost insurmountable, logistical and planning problems. The teams, operating under the strictest security precautions to preserve the element of surprise, would have to penetrate deep into Iran, enter the capital in some strength yet remain undetected, rescue the

hostages, who were dispersed in several different groups, and then carry out a withdrawal in the face of any number of possible Iranian military responses. Everyone recognised that transport, both in the air and on the ground, was the vital key. Unfortunately, Delta Force lacked its own transport capability, and outsiders, drawn from other units of the armed services, would have to be used.

## The rescuers would fly into Iran to carry the hostages out

Early plans involving insertions by parachute or by trucks driven to Tehran from Turkey were studied in detail and then rejected. Beckwith saw that long-range, heavy-lift helicopters would have to be used to fly the rescuers into Iran and to carry the hostages out. Carrier-based RH-53D Sea Stallions operated by the Marines fitted the bill, but despite their endurance, they could not reach Tehran in one hop – a refuelling stop somewhere in the desert south of the capital would have to be organised. Beckwith duly formulated a highly complex plan and, although he still had some nagging doubts about the ability of certain elements to perform their respective jobs, he remained confident that his plan would succeed.

Eagle Claw called for the various assault teams to fly at low

Above: Iranian Revolutionary Guards trample a US flag painted on a road. The Iranian revolution of 1978–79 was strongly anti-American. The United States had been the main support of the Shah of Iran's regime and was held responsible for the tyrannical aspects of the Shah's rule.

After the overthrow of the Shah in January 1979 a wave of anti-American feeling swept Iran. The United States, the chief supporter of the Shah while he was in power, was held responsible for the abuses of SAVAK (the regime's secret police) and as the source of the Western culture that was destroying the traditional Islamic society of Iran. When the exiled Shah visited the United States on 22 October 1979 for treatment of cancer, Iranian militants decided to strike directly at 'the Great Satan', the United States.

On 4 November approximately 400 students occupied the United States embassy in Tehran, and took 66 US citizens hostage. The militants demanded that to obtain the release of the hostages, the United States must return the Shah to Iran to stand trial. The Ayatollah Khomeini lent his support to this action. In the resulting turmoil, the government of Mehdi Bazargan, which had succeeded that of the Shah, collapsed. The Revolutionary Council – an umbrella organisation of groups opposed to the Shah and dominated by Islamic militants – then took control of the government, thereby eliminating any hope of an early release of the hostages. The Carter administration in the US was quick to react: the State Department formed an Iran working group on 4 November, and planning for a rescue operation began on 6 November. All Iranian financial assets held in the United States were frozen on 14 November.

level from Masirah to Desert One, an isolated spot in the Dasht-e-Karir some 300 miles southeast of Tehran, in three MC-130E transports. Three KC-130 tankers carrying fuel for the helicopters would also fly to Desert One. Once on the ground, a 12-man Road Watch Team would secure the landing strip, while Delta Force unloaded the rescue equipment. Some 30 minutes later, eight Sea Stallions, launched from the USS *Nimitz* stationed in the Gulf of Oman, would rendezvous at Desert One. After refuelling, the helicopters would take the 118-man rescue team towards a hide site nearer Tehran. After leaving Beckwith and his men, the RH-53s were then to proceed to a second hide site some 15 miles to the north and remain in hiding until called in to evacuate the hostages.

## The two assaults would go in simultaneously, through a hole blown in the compound wall

Delta Force would be met by two Department of Defense agents who would take the men to a wadi five miles from the landing zone, where they would spend the daylight hours in hiding. After sunset the agents would return with two vehicles: one to drive 12 men into Tehran to pick up the six transports to carry Delta into the capital; the other for

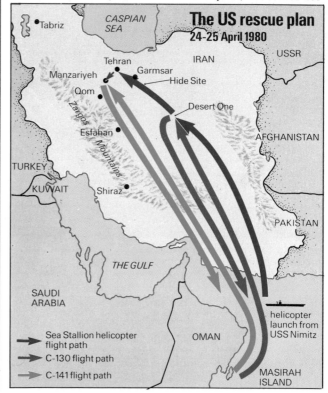

The US rescue plan
24-25 April 1980

Sea Stallion helicopter flight path
C-130 flight path
C-141 flight path

helicopter launch from USS Nimitz

Beckwith to undertake a final, on-the-spot reconnaissance of the route to the objective.

With the transport ready, Delta Force would begin the drive to Tehran at around 2030 hours on the second day. Beckwith had divided his command into three teams for the actual rescue mission – each had a specific objective. Red and Blue Elements, each 40 men strong, would provide the cutting edge: Red was to secure the western end of the embassy compound, take out any guards stationed in the motor pool or power plant, and free any hostages held in the staff college or commissary. Blue was to seize the southern sector of the compound and then rescue the prisoners held in the deputy chief of mission's residence, the ambassador's house and the chancellery. Outside the embassy, White Element's 13 men were to stop any Iranians from interfering with the operation and to cover the withdrawal.

The two assaults would go in simultaneously, after a massive explosion had blown a hole in the compound's outer wall. Meanwhile, a 13-man Special Forces team would storm the Foreign Ministry, where three hostages were being held separately from the main group. The various rescue attempts were expected to take place between 2300 and 2400 hours.

With the hostages freed, the Sea Stallions would be called in from their stand-by position somewhere to the north of Tehran, and, depending on the situation, would either land in the compound or in an adjacent sports stadium. Four AC-130E gunships would be available to deal with any Iranian response: one flying over Tehran to prevent Iranian troops from reaching the embassy, one over the nearest military airfield to discourage any airborne pursuit, and two in reserve to deal with any contingency.

Above: Colonel Charles Beckwith, first commander and founder of Delta Force. Colonel Beckwith had spent a year with the British SAS in 1962, as part of an exchange programme with the Special Forces. This inspired him to seek to form a similar type of unit within the US Army. In 1978, after several years of struggle with US Army bureaucracy, he achieved his aim. He retired from the Army in 1981.

## The pilots would fly blind into Tehran at ground lovol

Once aloft, the Sea Stallions were to fly with all speed to the airfield at Manzarieh, some 35 miles to the south of the capital. By this stage, the base would have been secured by a company of US Rangers flown in by C-130 Hercules transports, and three C-141 Starlifters would be on hand to fly out both the rescuers and the hostages. As there would be no chance of saving the Sea Stallions, they were to be destroyed and left behind.

In its final form, the plan was worryingly complex, and required several distinct forces to work in perfect unison. However, Beckwith had one over-riding concern: the helicopters. Their pilots would have to fly blind into Tehran at ground level to beat the radar defences, and any substantial losses would effectively end the mission. Although the planners had argued long and hard on the number of Sea Stallions required, all recognised that there had to be a minimum of six able to fly on to Tehran from Desert One; this number would guarantee sufficient capacity for all the hostages to be flown out.

Eagle Claw

Right: The burnt-out remains of
the KC-130 that blew up after a
Sea Stallion helicopter crashed
into it.
Below: The propeller of one of
the KC-130 engines.

Despite Beckwith's misgivings, the plan was given the presidential seal of approval, and Delta Force left its base at Fort Bragg in North Carolina, arriving at Masirah on 24 April. After last-minute checks over their equipment, the various assault teams, dressed in nondescript jeans, dust-covered brown boots and black combat jackets, boarded their MC-130Es at 1630 hours. One-and-a-half hours later, the first transport, containing Beckwith, Blue Element, the Road Watch Team and Colonel James Kyle (the air force officer in charge of operations at Desert One), was airborne, quickly followed by the other two transports and the three tankers.

## "The helicopters are launched. All eight got off." Everything was going according to plan

Flying on a northern course, the lead Hercules crossed into Iran near the town of Chah Bahar and dropped to 400ft for the low-level flight to Desert One. The Hercules was more than halfway to the preliminary objective when Kyle tapped Beckwith on the shoulder and said: 'The helicopters are launched. All eight got off.' Everything was going to plan, and at 2200 hours the first Hercules arrived over Desert One, flew a single circuit of the landing zone (LZ) and made a safe, if somewhat bumpy, landing.

With clockwork precision, the Road Watch Team left the cargo hold and raced off to secure the LZ's perimeter. All was quiet. Suddenly, headlights cut through the night sky, illuminating the transport. Beckwith shouted out, 'Stop that vehicle,' and opened fire. The vehicle, a Mercedes bus,

Above: One abandoned helicopter and the charred remains of another at Desert One. Two helicopters had already been lost when they encountered trouble while flying through a sandstorm. A third helicopter suffered a hydraulic systems failure and this led to the abandonment of Operation Eagle Claw.

After the failure of the hostage rescue mission of April 1980, both the United States and Iran waited for one or the other to indicate a willingness to negotiate the hostages' release. The death of the Shah on 27 July removed the obstacle of his return as a condition for the release of the hostages, and on 10 September the Iranian government notified the United States through diplomatic channels in West Germany that it wished to re-enter negotiations. All that the Iranians now demanded was the release of their frozen assets, the return of the Shah's assets and a US commitment not to interfere in Iranian affairs.

The Iraqi invasion of Iran, on 22 September, increased Iranian eagerness to achieve a settlement, as the hostage situation had lost the Iranians much international sympathy. The Iranian parliament, the Majlis, approved a resolution for the release of the hostages on 2 November. This resolution, however, was far from the US position on the intricate issue of claims which US citizens held against the Iranian government, so negotiations continued.

A general agreement for the release of the hostages was finally concluded on 16 January 1981.

The complicated financial arrangements involved in the release were not completed until 20 January, the day of Ronald Reagan's inauguration. The hostages themselves did not actually leave Iran until 12:33 pm on 20 January, and it was President Reagan who would greet them on their return.

screamed to a halt, and members of Blue Element surrounded it. At gunpoint, the 45 passengers were searched and placed under guard. No one had escaped; the mission remained uncompromised. However, over to the west of the LZ, a more serious incident was about to unfold. A second vehicle, a fuel tanker, hove into view. As the tanker, headlights ablaze, continued towards Desert One, it was taken out by a round fired from an M72 grenade launcher. Immediately, the night sky erupted with a vivid flash as its cargo of fuel exploded, illuminating the whole area. Worse, its driver escaped the inferno and made an unopposed getaway in a second vehicle. Although aware of this potentially disastrous turn of events, Beckwith ordered the mission to continue.

It was time for the other five Hercules to arrive. A few moments after the first troop-carrier had powered into the orange-black sky, on its return journey to Masirah, the second Hercules, with Red Element on board, made a perfect landing. After the aircraft was unloaded, its pilot taxied to a remote corner of the strip to make room for the remaining planes which arrived over the next few minutes. Once they were on the ground, the Hercules that had brought in Red Element took off for the return journey to Masirah. Everyone settled down to wait for the arrival of the eight Sea Stallions, scheduled to make the rendezvous in the next 30 minutes.

The helicopters were the key to the next phase of the mission and, at Desert One, Beckwith paced the desert like a caged tiger waiting for their arrival. Though he did not know it, the Sea Stallions had left the *Nimitz* dead on time, at 1930 hours. However, they were soon in trouble. At about 2145,

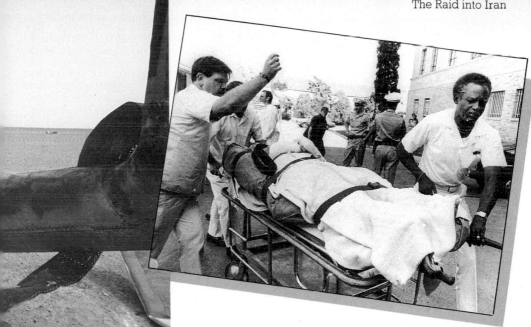

Above: An Iranian revolutionary guardsman gives the victory sign amid the wreckage.
The bodies of eight US servicemen were later displayed in Tehran as evidence of the failure of American schemes.
Above right: Five US servicemen were injured at Desert One, suffering burns. They were flown back to the United States for treatment.

No.6 helicopter was forced to make a landing due to irreparable mechanical problems. Its crew was picked up, but now only seven choppers could make it to Desert One. The margin for error allowed by the planners was already being eroded.

## The Sea Stallions ran into two unexpected sandstorms

The remaining Sea Stallions were also having problems after running into two totally unexpected and vicious sandstorms. The one flown by the force commander, Major Seiffert, and No.2 chopper made forced landings to ride out the worst of the storms. Luckily, after over 20 minutes on the ground, the storms passed and both crews resumed their journeys to Desert One. However, No.5 Sea Stallion suffered a major mechanical failure and, unable to carry on with the mission, was forced to return to the *Nimitz*. There was no longer any margin for error.

The first helicopter to reach Desert One, No.3, arrived 50 minutes late, guided in by the burning fuel tanker; the remaining five straggled in over the next 30 minutes. Despite the delay, there was still a chance that Delta could reach the hide site before first light. However, Beckwith was informed that No.2 helicopter was all but inoperable, and that left only five choppers serviceable. After a quick discussion with Kyle, who contacted senior military officials monitoring the operation in Egypt, it was decided that the raid was no longer feasible. Beckwith ordered his men to load their equipment on the Sea Stallions. The daring attempt to free the embassy hostages had been forced to abort because of the systems failure of a complicated piece of machinery. Courage alone could count for little in this situation.

However, before Delta could depart, No.4 helicopter needed refuelling. Only one tanker had any spare fuel, and to make way for the helicopter, No.3 Sea Stallion had to be moved. Overloaded, the chopper shuddered into the air, attempted to bank, failed, and crashed into the fuel tanker. The effect was instantaneous and wholly catastrophic: the two machines erupted in flames, covering the area with red-hot debris. Five crewmen in the Hercules died instantly, as did three Marines in the chopper; the Delta men in the tanker were lucky to escape with their lives. Beckwith had no choice but to get his men onto the remaining transports and evacuate Desert One. After nearly five hours on Iranian soil, Delta Force returned to Masirah.

## The blame lay with mechanical problems and freak sandstorms

The mission was an undoubted failure – the hostages would not, in the event, be released until January 1981 – but Delta Force could not be held responsible. The blame lay with the combination of unfortunate mechanical problems and the onset of freak sandstorms. Without these disastrous set-backs, the US hostage crisis might have ended in April, and the men of Delta Force would certainly have been acclaimed as heroes. Operation Eagle Claw taught the US Special Forces a number of grim lessons that would not quickly be forgotten.

Below: The newly-released hostages from the American Embassy in Tehran received a ticker-tape parade down New York City's Fifth Avenue. It was not until January 1981, nine months after Operation Eagle Claw, that the hostages were finally released, after lengthy negotiations between Iran and the United States.

# 7

# THE MODERN ROLE
## Anti-terrorist Watchdogs

In July 1985 US Special Forces consisted of four Special Forces Groups (Airborne) – SFGAs – with another four groups in the Army Reserves. Each SFGA consists of 776 men divided into three battalions. The 1st SFGA is based at Fort Lewis, Washington, the 5th SFGA and 7th SFGA are based at Fort Bragg, North Carolina, and the 10th SFGA is based at Fort Devens, Massachusetts. Current overseas deployment consists of: the 3rd Battalion, 7th SFGA, permanently stationed in Panama; the 1st Battalion, 1st SFGA, stationed on Okinawa, Japan; and the 1st Battalion, 10th SFGA, stationed in Bad Tolz, West Germany. There are also Special Forces detachments in El Salvador, Honduras, South Korea and Berlin. The composition of both the South Korea and Berlin detachments is secret but the Berlin unit is known to be a special force trained to go underground and disrupt Soviet operations should Soviet forces overrun the city.

'ANYTHING, ANYTIME, Anywhere, Anyhow', the bold motto of the US Special Forces, is as true a description of the role of the Green Berets today as it was of the work of their predecessors, the 1st Special Service Force of World War II and the behind-the-lines 'A-Teams' operating in the jungles of Vietnam. Known variously as 'Sneaky Petes' and 'snake eaters', the men of the Special Forces have always been earmarked for the 'dirty' jobs – jobs that require certain types of skill and, to carry them out, a special breed of soldier. But ever since the Green Berets were first raised as part of the US military establishment, their fortunes have been subject to the contemporary military climate in Washington and this has not always been to their advantage.

## With America at peace, it seemed the 'snake eaters' were not needed

During the Vietnam conflict the Green Berets had a war to fight, and, despite considerable friction with the 'regular' military, they played an important part in the guerrilla-style warfare that characterised that campaign. However, when the last Green Beret units were withdrawn from Vietnam in March 1971, the Special Forces were faced with an unsettled future as their covert role, working behind enemy lines, became redundant. From a wartime high in 1969 of some 13,000 men, the Special Forces' manpower levels were drastically reduced to 3000 by 1980, as group after group was deactivated. Cuts in men were matched by cuts in finance and, with America at peace, it seemed that the 'snake eaters' were no longer needed.

While the Special Forces kept a low profile during the

Page 87: Armed with a Colt Commando, a member of the Special Forces continues the exhaustive training that keeps the Green Berets at peak efficiency.
Above: A member of the Special Forces during Operation Bright Star in Egypt.
Far left: Sergeant Raymond Beauscher of the 5th Special Forces Group rappels from an army helicopter 105ft above ground. Such skills are useful for operating in mountain areas or behind enemy lines.
Above left: A whole Green Beret team rappels from a helicopter.

1970s, however, a new threat was emerging – an escalation in international terrorist activity. All over the world aircraft were being hijacked and hostages taken, and many countries began to look to their special forces for a military solution to the problem. The massacre of 9 Israeli athletes in a shoot-out at the 1972 Munich Olympics highlighted the dangers of deploying regular units against terrorist groups, and soon the short, sharp application of force by a small detachment of intensively trained men became the accepted approach. While Britain has the Special Air Service Regiment, and Germany has created GSG9 to combat the threat, America turned to the Green Berets, whose particular brand of fighting skills are admirably suited to this type of work. On 20 July 1978, the 1st Special Forces Operational Detachment D, better known as Delta Force, was formed for the specific purpose of meeting the new requirement.

The Pentagon's revived interest in the Green Berets and special operations units in general was not satisfied, however, with the creation of Delta. To the US administration in the 1980s another potentially explosive factor has emerged to

The varied skills of the Green Berets are honed by constant training, especially by exercises at the Special Forces School at Fort Bragg in North Carolina where this series of photographs was taken.
Above: Two members of A-Team 743 take stock of terrain from a defensive position.
Above right: More members of the 7th Special Forces Group prepare demolition charges. (Note the AK-47 carried by the soldier on the left.)
Right: Further members of A-Team 743 familiarise themselves with new communications equipment.
Far right: Master Sergeant George Sandy jumps an 'enemy' during close combat training at Fort Bragg.

be added to the terrorist threat – a perceived increase in the level of Soviet and Cuban support to guerrilla movements in the Third World countries of Africa, Latin America, the Caribbean and Southeast Asia. This support consists of direct military aid in the form of modern-weapons shipments and the provision of military advisory teams to organise and train anti-government guerrilla forces. The Soviet invasion of Afghanistan in 1979 and intelligence reports on the strengthening of Soviet Spetsnaz special forces have further fuelled the growing demand for military forces capable of dealing with what have become known as 'low-intensity' conflicts. As a 1983 report commissioned by the US Army stated: 'We have come to realise that we cannot slug it out with nuclear weapons and we must prepare for an era when low-intensity conflict is the norm.' Dealing with peacetime 'instability' in the Third World, where the deployment of large, regular forces is politically impossible, has now become the central concern of the Special Forces. In this role it is the job of the Green Berets to be ready at all times for rapid deployment at a moment's notice anywhere in the world, either as a shock force or as a military advisory mission.

## 'In the 1st Special Operations Command we are not patting ourselves on the back...'

After the failure of Delta Force's attempt to rescue the US hostages held in the American embassy in Tehran in 1980, the US military set about reassessing the future role and deployment of its special units. The Reagan administration's hard line on Soviet expansion in the Third World, especially in Central America, the US 'backyard', has placed Special

Forces' expansion high on the US list of military priorities. As a result, on 1 October 1982, the army set up the 1st Special Operations Command (SOCOM) at Fort Bragg, the home of the Green Berets in North Carolina. SOCOM is charged with standardising training throughout army special units and is responsible for the preparation and deployment of all US army special operations units including the Green Berets. SOCOM's first CO, Major-General Joseph C. Lutz, describes the new command:

In July 1985 US Special Operations Forces (SOFs) consisted of elite units from the army, navy and air force. Army SOFs comprised: four SFGAs, three Ranger battalions, the 96th Civil Affairs Battalion, one Psyop Group, Delta Force, and the 160th Task Force of the 101st Army Air Assault Division. The combined total of personnel on active service was 9100. The navy fielded two Special Warfare Groups consisting of six navy SEAL Teams, three Special Warfare Units, two Special Boat Squadrons, two Special Boat Units and two SEAL Delivery Vehicle Teams. Navy personnel totalled 1700. The air force SOFs were organised under the 23rd Air Force Special Operations Wing made up of five squadrons and a helicopter detachment. A total of 4100 personnel were assigned to the air force SOF complement.

Between 1986 and 1990 substantial increases in the SOFs are planned both in manpower and in specialist technical equipment.

'In the 1st Special Operations Command we are not sitting around patting ourselves on the back because our value has apparently been recognised. On the contrary, special operations forces (SOFs) will never be more than modest in size. To accomplish the mission set before us, however, our soldiers must be extraordinarily professional. We are working at the business of integrating all elements of the new command into a cohesive professional force...'

Recognition by the US Army and support for the Special Forces from the Reagan administration quickly resulted in a boost to Special Forces' manpower levels. In January 1984 Washington announced the urgent necessity for the expansion of American anti-guerrilla forces, and on 15 March the first battalion of the 1st Special Forces Group (Airborne) was reactivated at Fort Bragg and deployed to Okinawa in the Far East. In September the remaining two battalions of the 776-man group were reactivated and based at Fort Lewis, Washington. To supplement the four existing groups (the 1st, 5th, 7th and 10th SFGs), another new group will have come into service by 1990.

Progress in the revitalisation of the SOFs continued apace, and on 1 January 1984 the Joint Special Operations Agency (JSOA) was created to oversee the expansion of specialist units across three branches of the armed forces. Apart from the Green Berets, the SOFs also include a psychological warfare (psyops) group, a civil affairs battalion, three Ranger battalions, US Navy SEAL (Sea, Air, Land) Teams, and various special air force units. Under the JSOA, the various specialist skills of army, navy and air force personnel can be coordinated to maximum effect and are constantly at hand for rapid deployment.

Despite the changes in command structure on the higher level and the gathering together of America's elite units under the umbrella of a joint agency, the traditional role of the Green Berets as counter-insurgency and counter-revolutionary warfare fighters remains at the core of the Special Forces concept. Training of Special Forces is still just as tough, and in their global strategic role personnel must be able to operate and fight in any conditions. Airborne

Below: Training with scuba gear. Although many members of the Special Forces have acquired this skill, it is not compulsory. The US Navy SEALS are considered to be the prime formation to undertake underwater activities.

Left: Preparing for a parachute jump. All Special Forces personnel are airborne-qualified.
Below: Living off the land requires mental as well as physical toughness. The Green Berets were nicknamed 'snake eaters' in Vietnam.

qualification is a basic requirement, and training continues in the use of more than 80 different weapon types, with special emphasis on the handling of foreign equipment. Exercises are held in desert, jungle, Arctic and temperate environments, and troops attend courses to train as engineering, communications, intelligence, medical and firearms specialists.

The Green Berets, along with the other SOFs, today form the cutting edge of the US armed forces. Whether used as storm troops in a hostage rescue mission, as military training teams in a low-intensity conflict, or as the 'guerrilla' element in any future open conflict, the Green Berets remain an important and very active element in the US order of battle.

# CHRONOLOGY

**1952** The 10th Special Forces Group (Airborne) – SFG (Airborne) – is activated at Fort Bragg, North Carolina, under the command of Colonel Aaron Bank.

**1953** The 77th SFG (Airborne) is activated. The 10th SFG (Airborne) is sent to serve in NATO forces at Bad Tölz, West Germany.

**1957** The 1st SFG (Airborne) is activated. Members of 1st SFG (Airborne) are sent to South Vietnam to train commando units for the Army of the Republic of Vietnam.

**1959** Members of the 77th SFG (Airborne) are sent to Laos to train the Royal Laotian Army. Army Reserve and National Guard special forces units are formed.

**1960** The 77th SFG (Airborne) is renamed the 7th SFG (Airborne).

**1961** The 5th SFG (Airborne) is formed in South Vietnam. The Area Development Program is begun.

**1962** The Area Development Program is renamed the Civilian Irregular Defense Group (CIDG) Program.

**1963** The 3rd, 6th and 8th SFGs (Airborne) are activated.

**1964** The Studies and Observation Group, an unconventional warfare task force, is formed. Project Delta is begun.

**1965** The Mobile Strike Forces are formed.

**1966** Projects Omega and Sigma are begun.

**1969** The 3rd SFG (Airborne) is deactivated. The 10th SFG (Airborne) moves from West Germany to Fort Devens, Massachusetts.

**1970** Special Forces units begin to pull out of Southeast Asia. The Civilian Irregular Defense Group (CIDG) Program is terminated.

**1971** The 6th SFG (Airborne) is deactivated.

**1972** The 8th SFG (Airborne) is deactivated.

**1973** The Studies and Observation Group is disbanded.

**1974** The 1st SFG (Airborne) is deactivated.

**1978** Special Forces Operational Detachment Delta (Delta Force) is activated for counter-terrorist missions.

**1980** Delta Force attempts to rescue the Iranian Embassy hostages.

**1982** The 1st Special Forces Operational Command is formed.

**1983** Delta Force participates in the invasion of Grenada.

**1984** The 1st SFG (Airborne) is reactivated.

# FURTHER READING

Beckwith, Col. Charlie A., US Army (ret.), and Knox, Donald, *Delta Force,* Arms and Armour Press, London 1984

Eshel, David, *Elite Fighting Units,* Arco Publishing, New York 1984

Rottman, Gordon L., *US Army Special Forces 1952–84*, Osprey Publishing, London 1985

Simpson, Charles M., *Inside the Green Berets*, Arms and Armour Press, London 1983

Stanton, Shelby L., *Vietnam Order of Battle*, US News & World, New York 1982

# INDEX

Page numbers in *italics* refer to illustrations. The following abbreviations are used: Div = Division, Bde = Brigade, Btn = Battalion, Sqn = Squadron.